DEDICATION

..IN MEMORY OF GRANPA TUTBURY,
WHO RAN OFF LAST CHRISTMAS
TO JOIN A SWARM OF "KILLER BEES,"
ALL OF WHICH IS RATHER ENIGMATIC,
SINCE GRAMPS NEVER HAD A
SWEET TOOTH NOR SHOWED A
PREFERENCE FOR SWARMING.

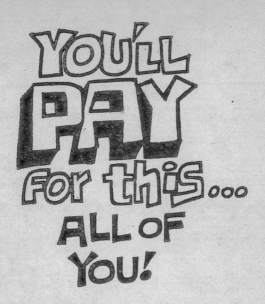

YOU'LL PAY for this... ALL OF YOU!

by Parker, Rechin
and Wilder

FAWCETT GOLD MEDAL • NEW YORK

YOU'LL PAY FOR THIS... ALL OF YOU!

A Fawcett Gold Medal Book published by arrangement with Fiel
Newspaper Syndicate.

ISBN: 0-449-14121-7

Printed in the United States of America .

10 9 8 7 6 5 4 3 2 1

monday

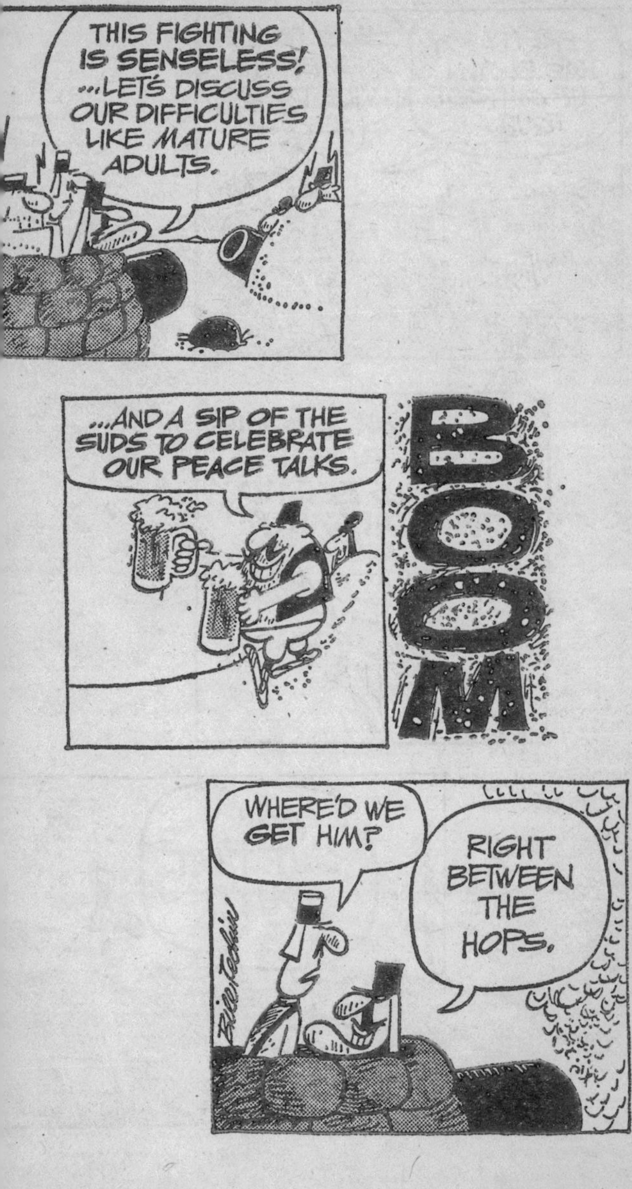
THIS FIGHTING IS SENSELESS! ...LET'S DISCUSS OUR DIFFICULTIES LIKE MATURE ADULTS.
...AND A SIP OF THE SUDS TO CELEBRATE OUR PEACE TALKS.
BOOM
WHERE'D WE GET HIM?
RIGHT BETWEEN THE HOPS.

tuesday

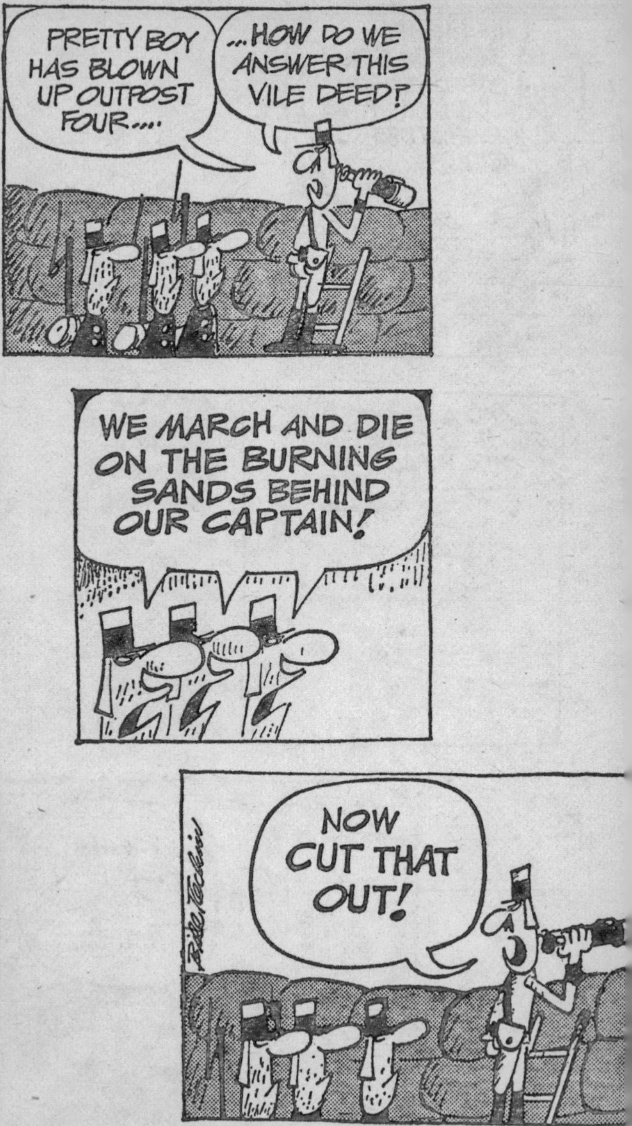
PRETTY BOY HAS BLOWN UP OUTPOST FOUR....
...HOW DO WE ANSWER THIS VILE DEED?
WE MARCH AND DIE ON THE BURNING SANDS BEHIND OUR CAPTAIN!
NOW CUT THAT OUT!

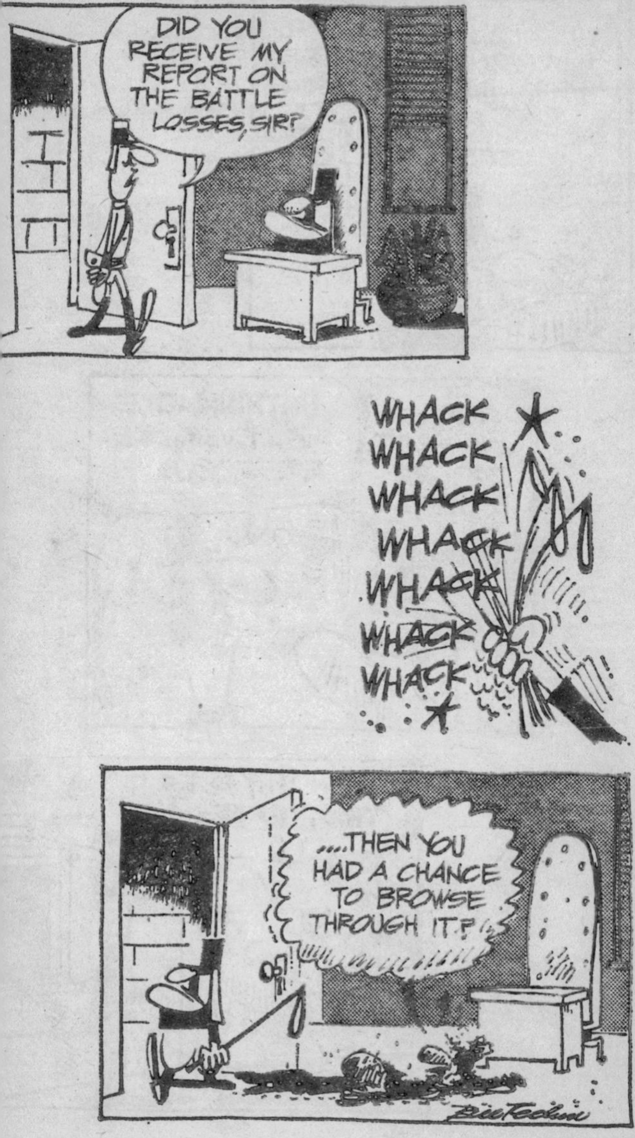
DID YOU RECEIVE MY REPORT ON THE BATTLE LOSSES, SIR?
WHACK
WHACK
WHACK
WHACK
WHACK
WHACK
WHACK
....THEN YOU HAD A CHANCE TO BROWSE THROUGH IT.?

thursday

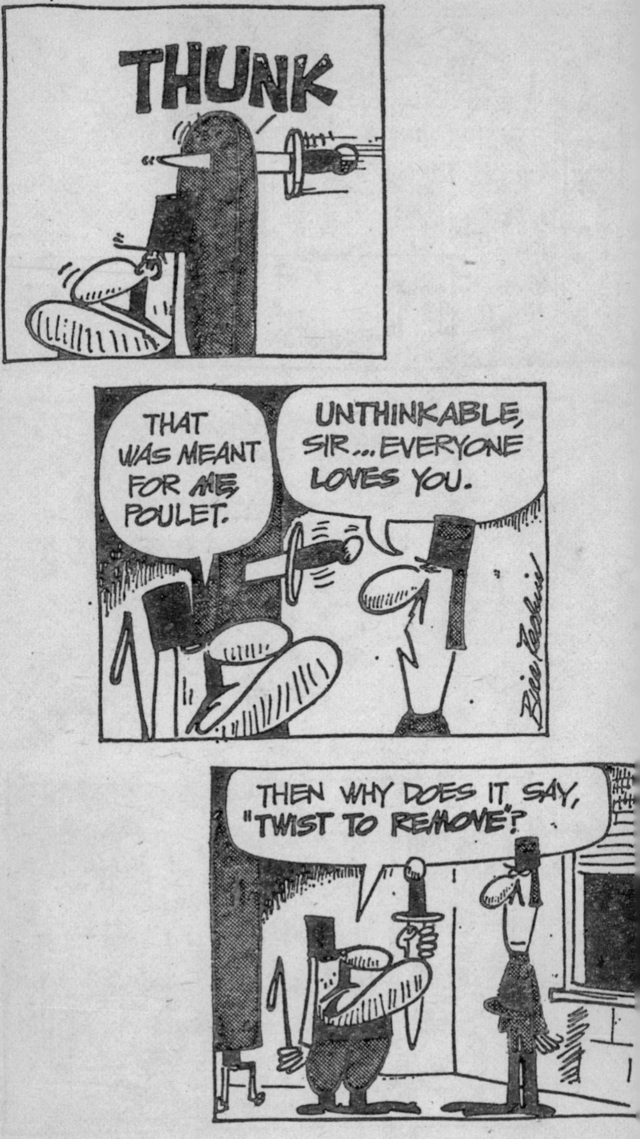
THUNK
THAT WAS MEANT FOR ME, POULET.
UNTHINKABLE, SIR... EVERYONE LOVES YOU.
THEN WHY DOES IT SAY, "TWIST TO REMOVE"?

friday

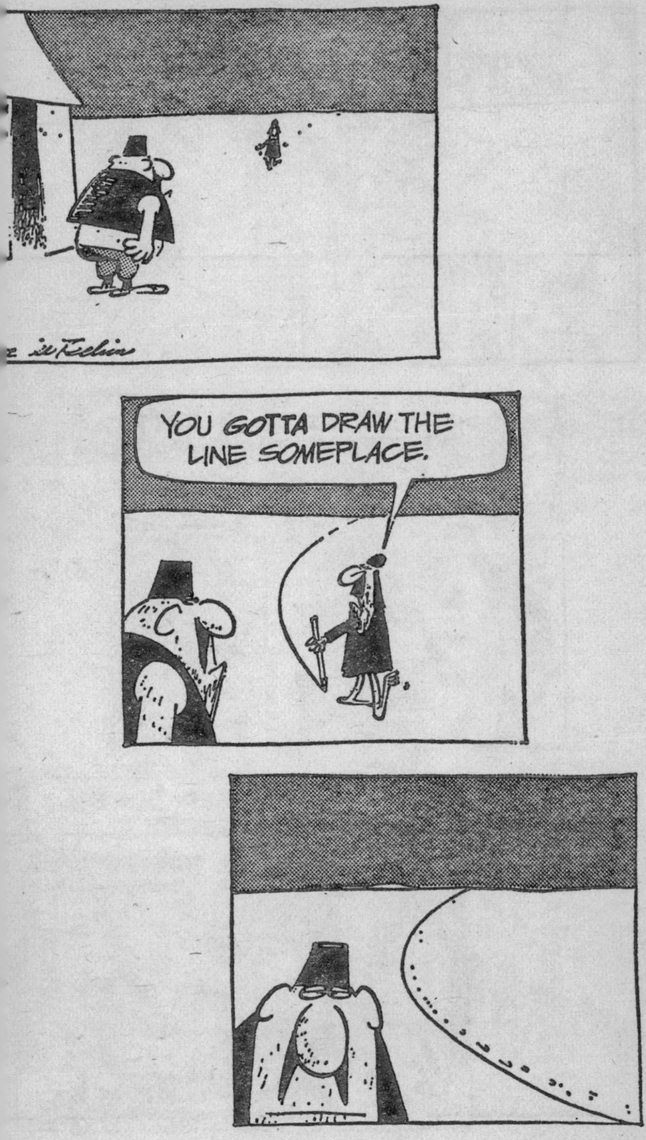
YOU GOTTA DRAW THE LINE SOMEPLACE.

saturday

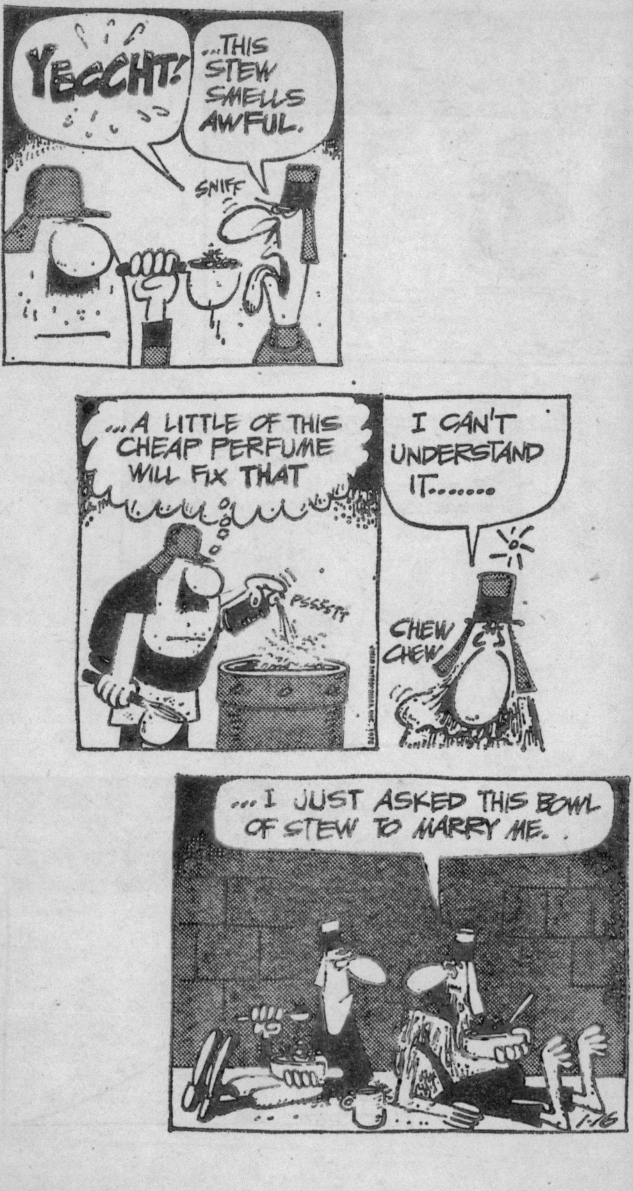
YECCHT!
...THIS STEW SMELLS AWFUL.
SNIFF
...A LITTLE OF THIS CHEAP PERFUME WILL FIX THAT
PSSSSTT
I CAN'T UNDERSTAND IT.......
CHEW CHEW
...I JUST ASKED THIS BOWL OF STEW TO MARRY ME.
1-16

monday

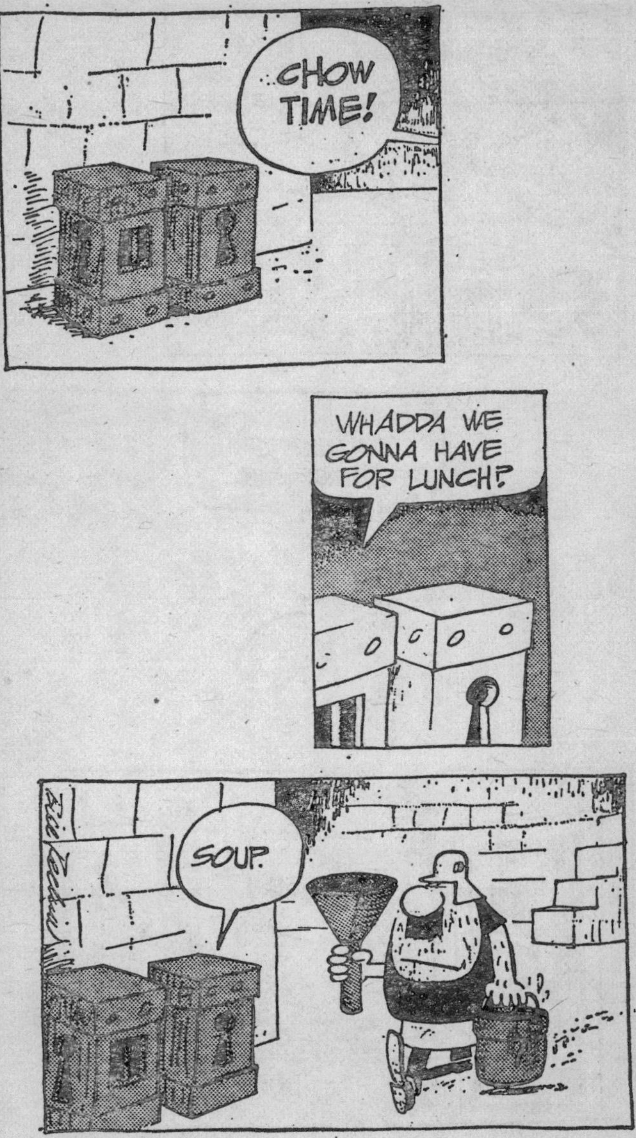
CHOW TIME!
WHADDA WE GONNA HAVE FOR LUNCH?
SOUP.

tuesday

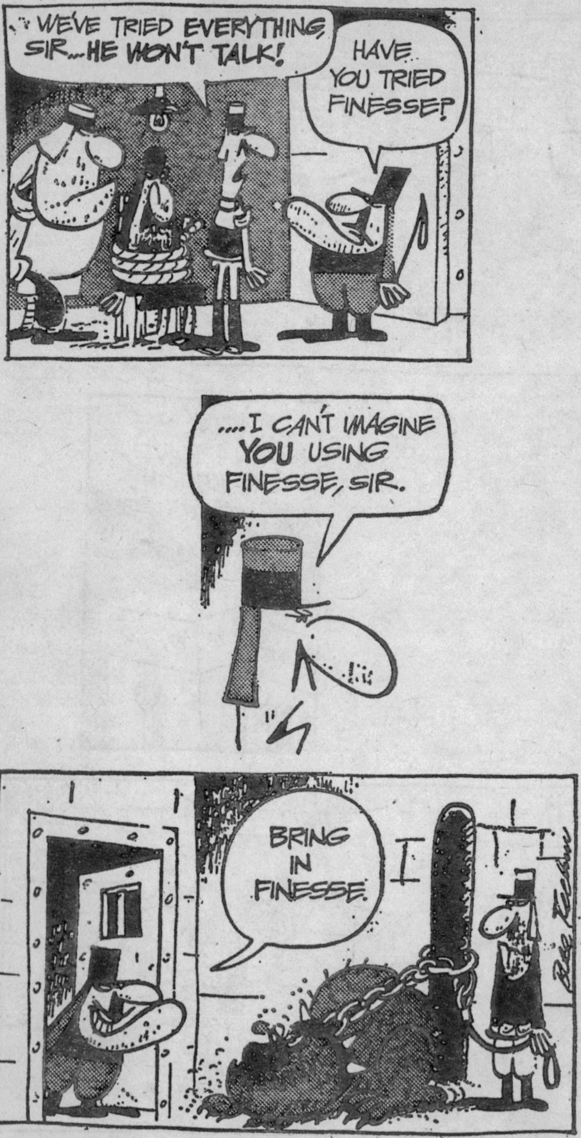
WE'VE TRIED EVERYTHING, SIR...HE WON'T TALK!
HAVE YOU TRIED FINESSE?
....I CAN'T IMAGINE YOU USING FINESSE, SIR.
BRING IN FINESSE.

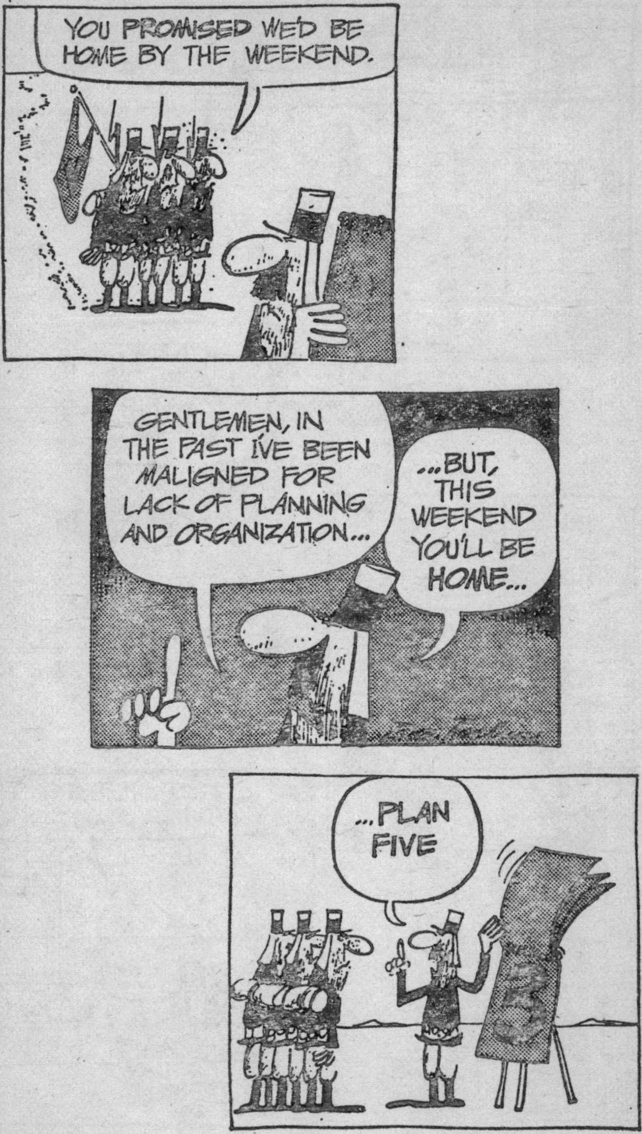
YOU PROMISED WE'D BE HOME BY THE WEEKEND.
GENTLEMEN, IN THE PAST I'VE BEEN MALIGNED FOR LACK OF PLANNING AND ORGANIZATION...
...BUT, THIS WEEKEND YOU'LL BE HOME...
...PLAN FIVE

thursday

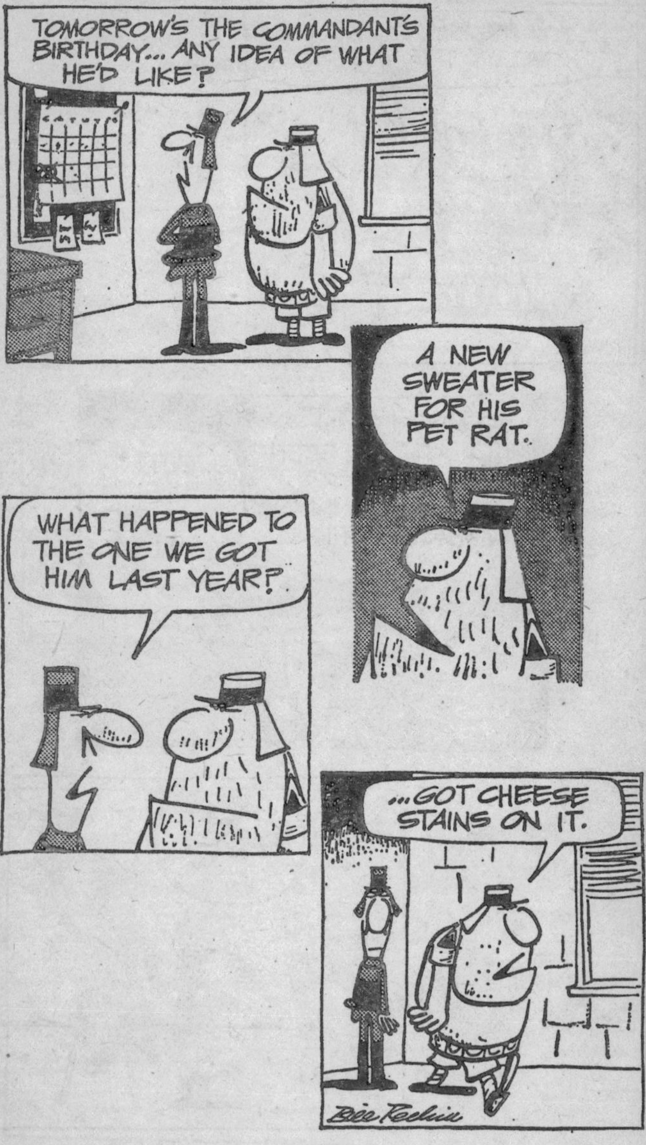
TOMORROW'S THE COMMANDANT'S BIRTHDAY... ANY IDEA OF WHAT HE'D LIKE?
A NEW SWEATER FOR HIS PET RAT.
WHAT HAPPENED TO THE ONE WE GOT HIM LAST YEAR?
...GOT CHEESE STAINS ON IT.
Bill Rechin

friday

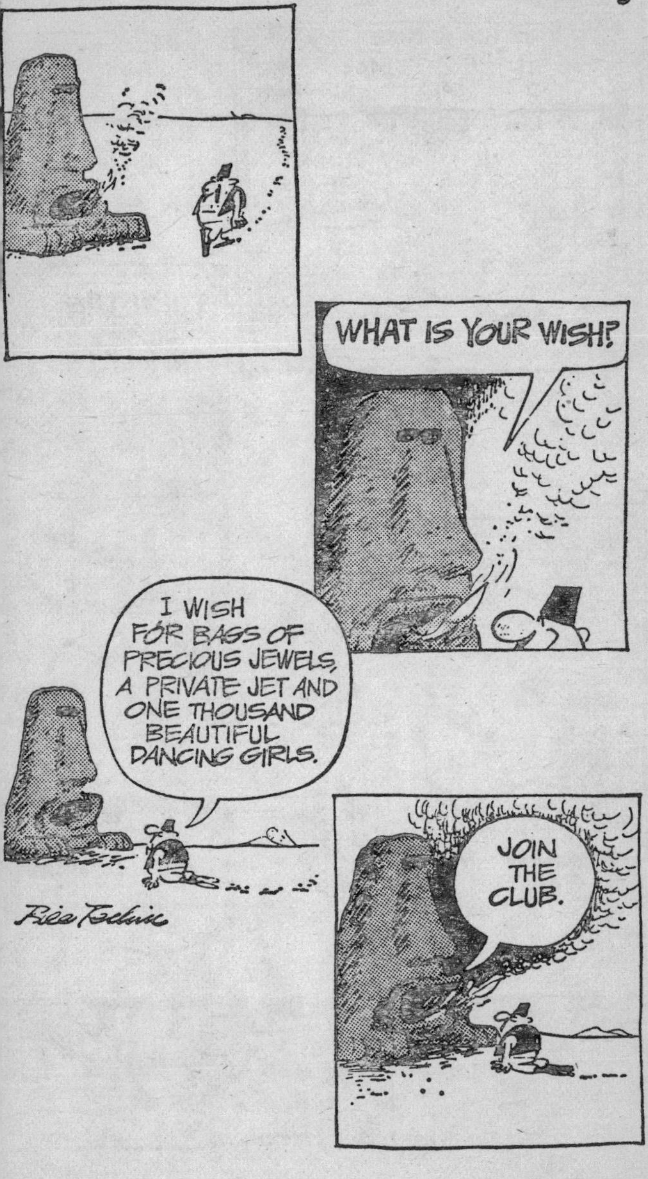
WHAT IS YOUR WISH?
I WISH FOR BAGS OF PRECIOUS JEWELS, A PRIVATE JET AND ONE THOUSAND BEAUTIFUL DANCING GIRLS.
JOIN THE CLUB.

saturday

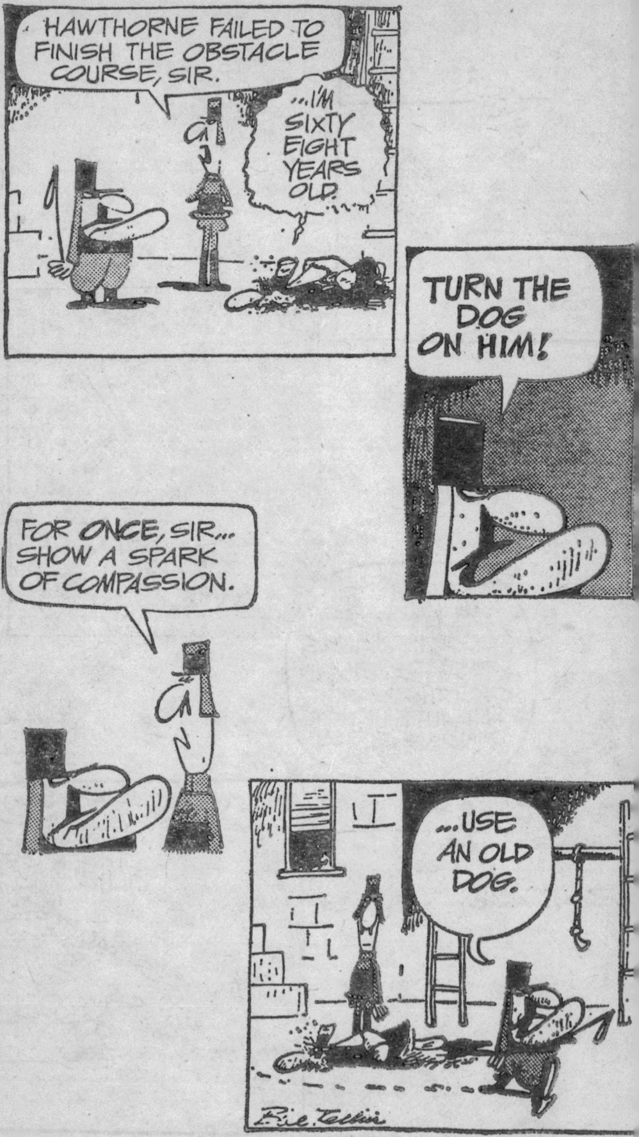
HAWTHORNE FAILED TO FINISH THE OBSTACLE COURSE, SIR.
...I'M SIXTY EIGHT YEARS OLD.
TURN THE DOG ON HIM!
FOR ONCE, SIR... SHOW A SPARK OF COMPASSION.
...USE AN OLD DOG.

monday

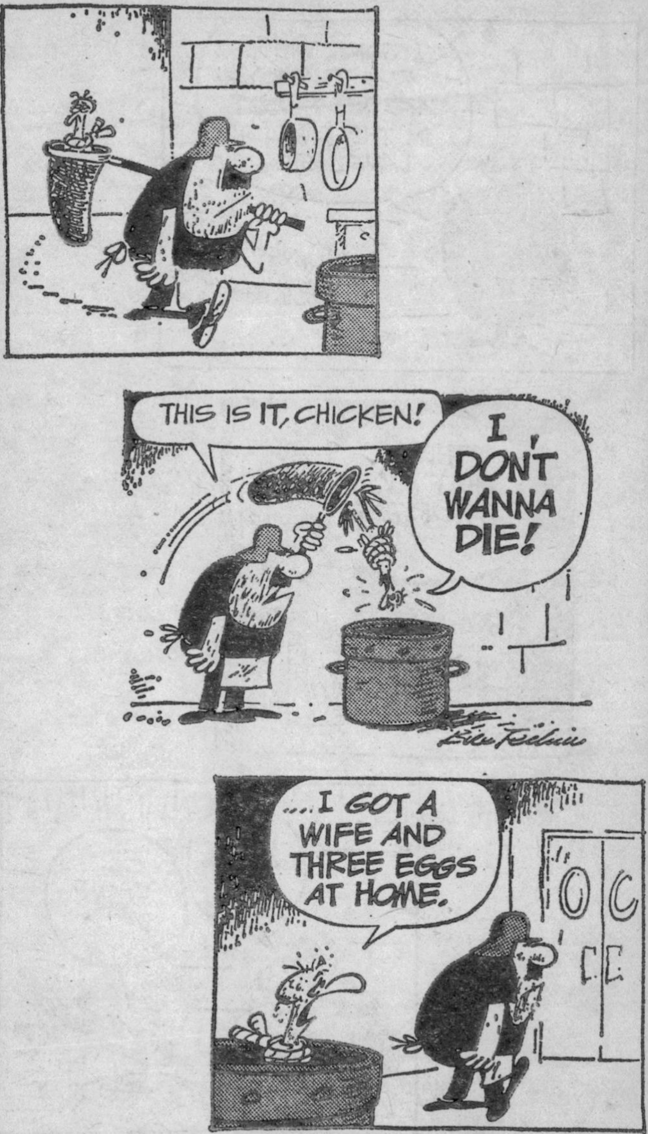
THIS IS IT, CHICKEN!
I DON'T WANNA DIE!
....I GOT A WIFE AND THREE EGGS AT HOME.

tuesday

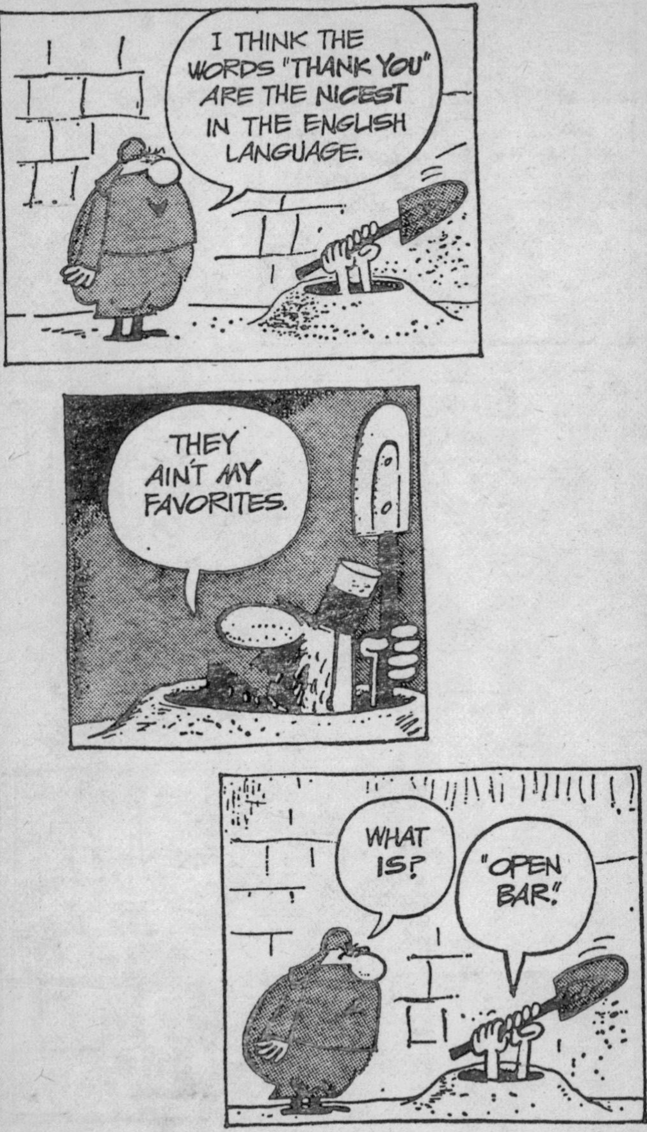
I THINK THE WORDS "THANK YOU" ARE THE NICEST IN THE ENGLISH LANGUAGE.
THEY AIN'T MY FAVORITES.
WHAT IS?
"OPEN BAR."

wednesday

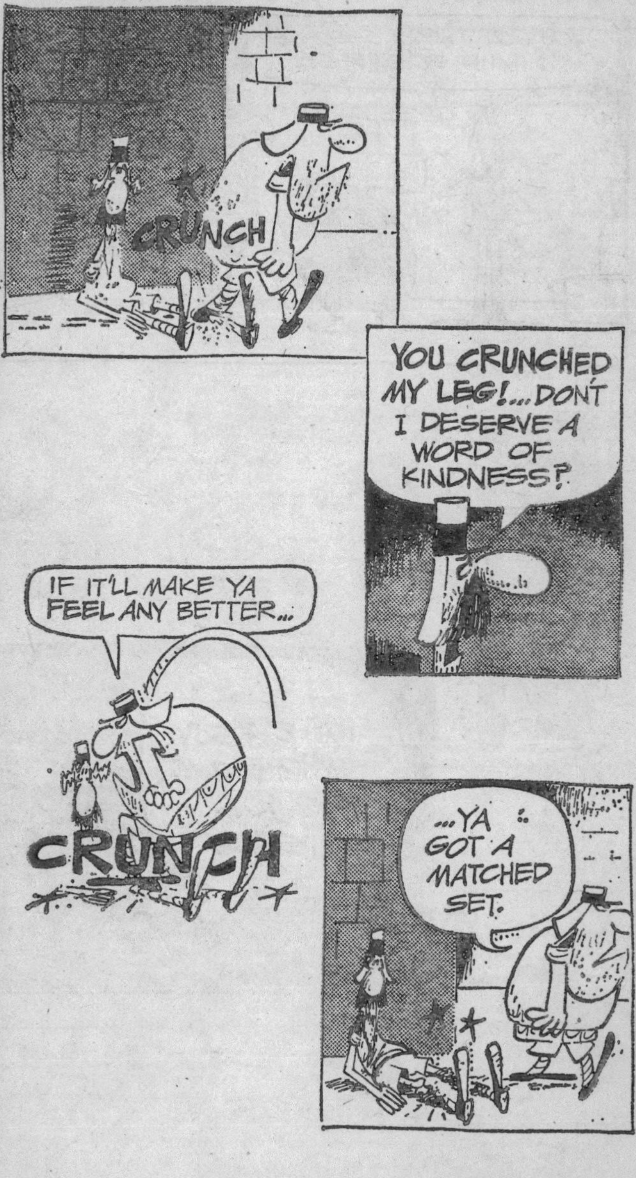
CRUNCH
YOU CRUNCHED MY LEG!...DON'T I DESERVE A WORD OF KINDNESS?
IF IT'LL MAKE YA FEEL ANY BETTER...
CRUNCH
...YA GOT A MATCHED SET.

thursday

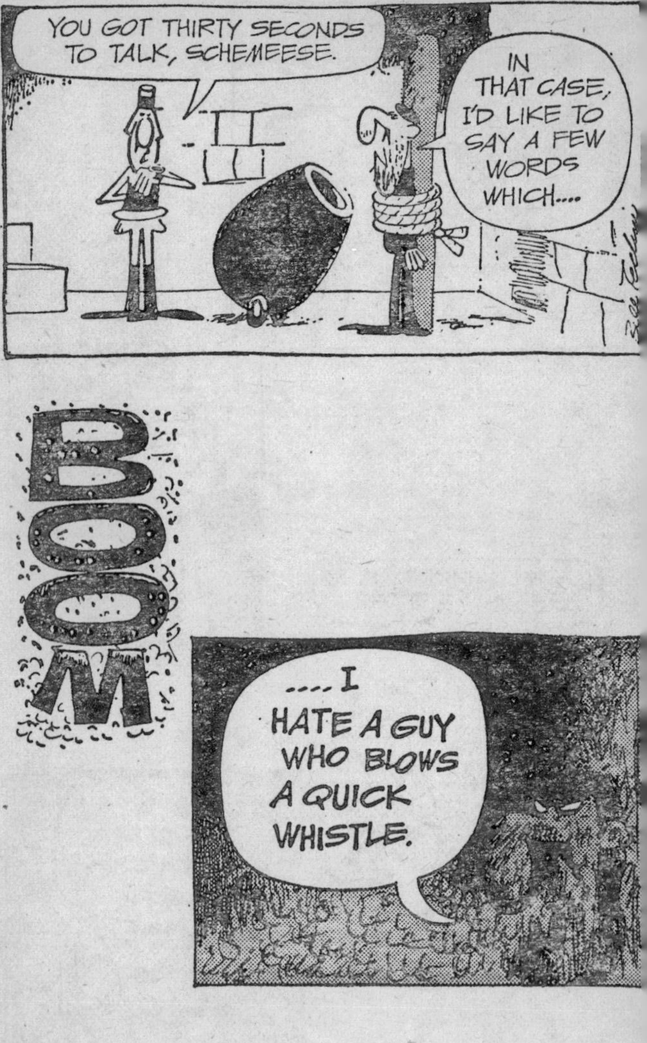
YOU GOT THIRTY SECONDS TO TALK, SCHEMEESE.
IN THAT CASE, I'D LIKE TO SAY A FEW WORDS WHICH....
BOOM
.... I HATE A GUY WHO BLOWS A QUICK WHISTLE.

friday

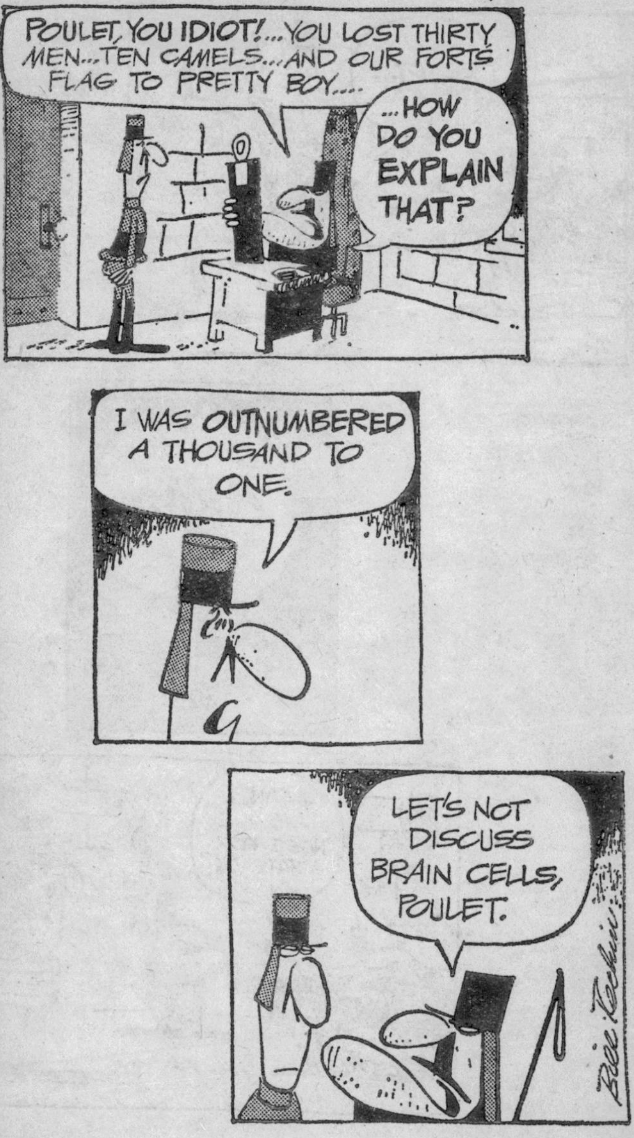
POULET, YOU IDIOT!...YOU LOST THIRTY MEN...TEN CAMELS...AND OUR FORT'S FLAG TO PRETTY BOY....
...HOW DO YOU EXPLAIN THAT?
I WAS OUTNUMBERED A THOUSAND TO ONE.
LET'S NOT DISCUSS BRAIN CELLS, POULET.

saturday

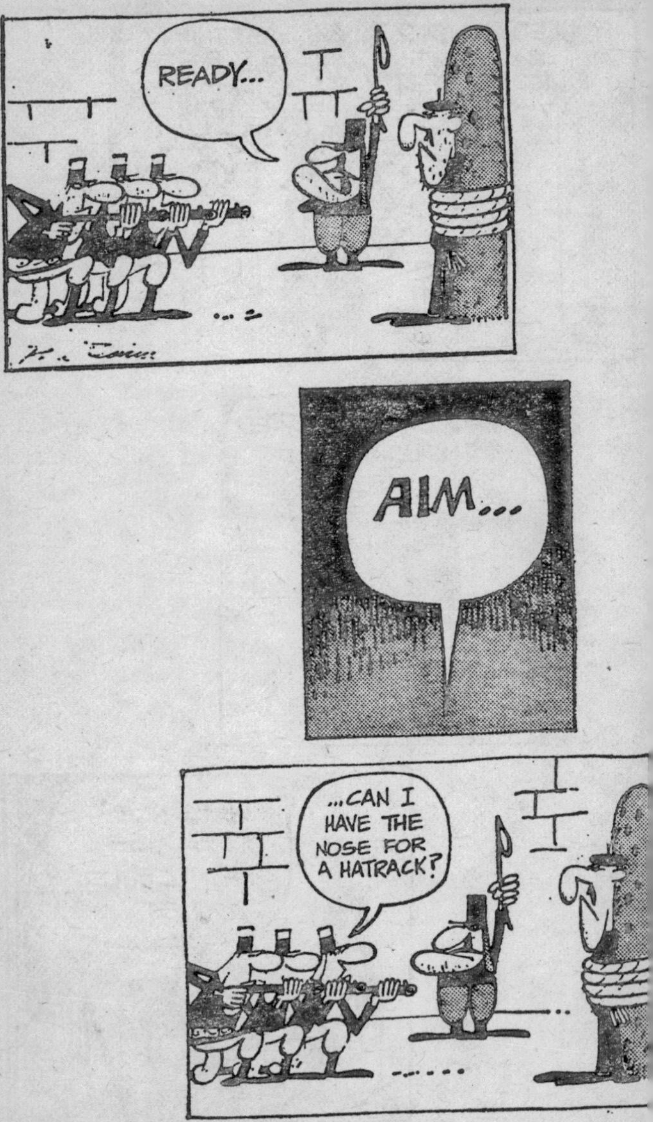
READY...
AIM...
...CAN I HAVE THE NOSE FOR A HATRACK?

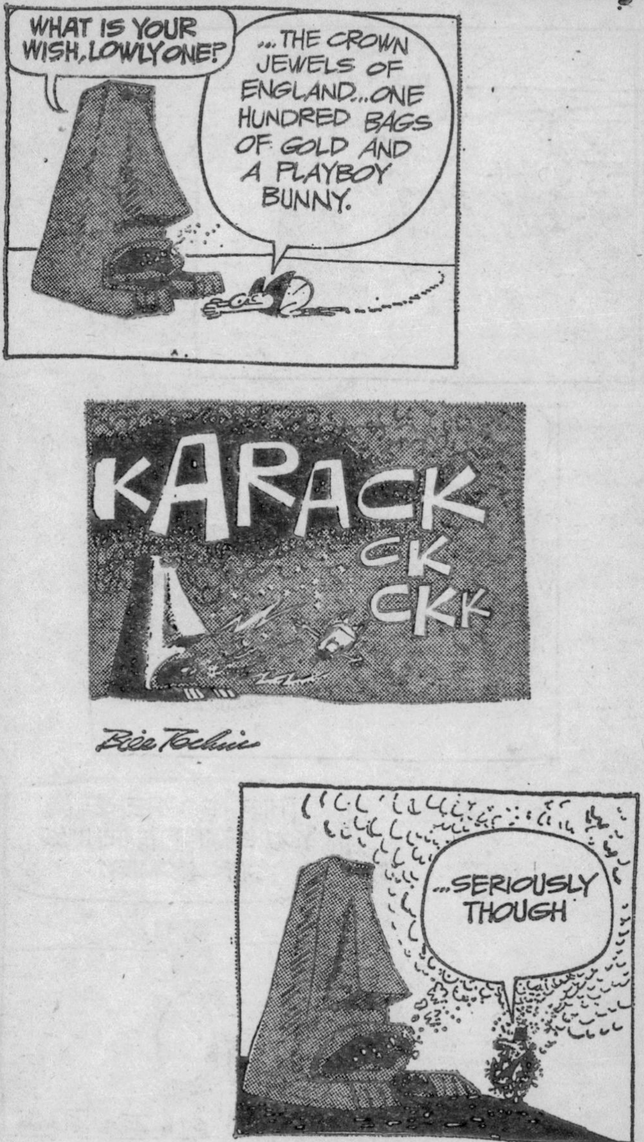
WHAT IS YOUR WISH, LOWLY ONE?
...THE CROWN JEWELS OF ENGLAND...ONE HUNDRED BAGS OF GOLD AND A PLAYBOY BUNNY.
KARACK
CK
CKK
...SERIOUSLY THOUGH

tuesday

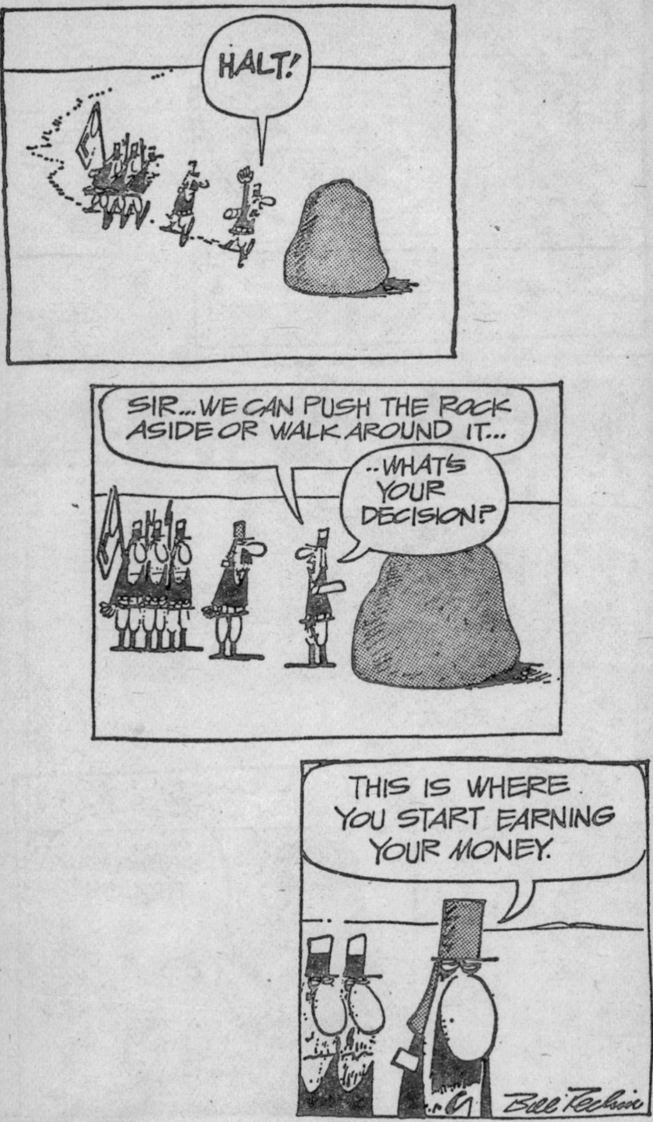
HALT!
SIR...WE CAN PUSH THE ROCK ASIDE OR WALK AROUND IT...
..WHAT'S YOUR DECISION?
THIS IS WHERE YOU START EARNING YOUR MONEY.
Bill Rechin

wednesday

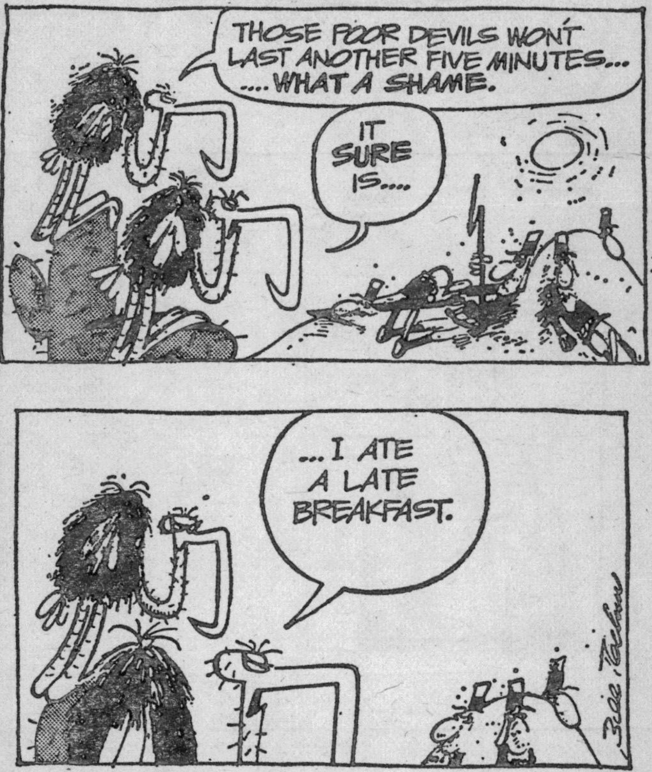
THOSE POOR DEVILS WON'T LAST ANOTHER FIVE MINUTES... ....WHAT A SHAME.
IT SURE IS....
...I ATE A LATE BREAKFAST.

thursday

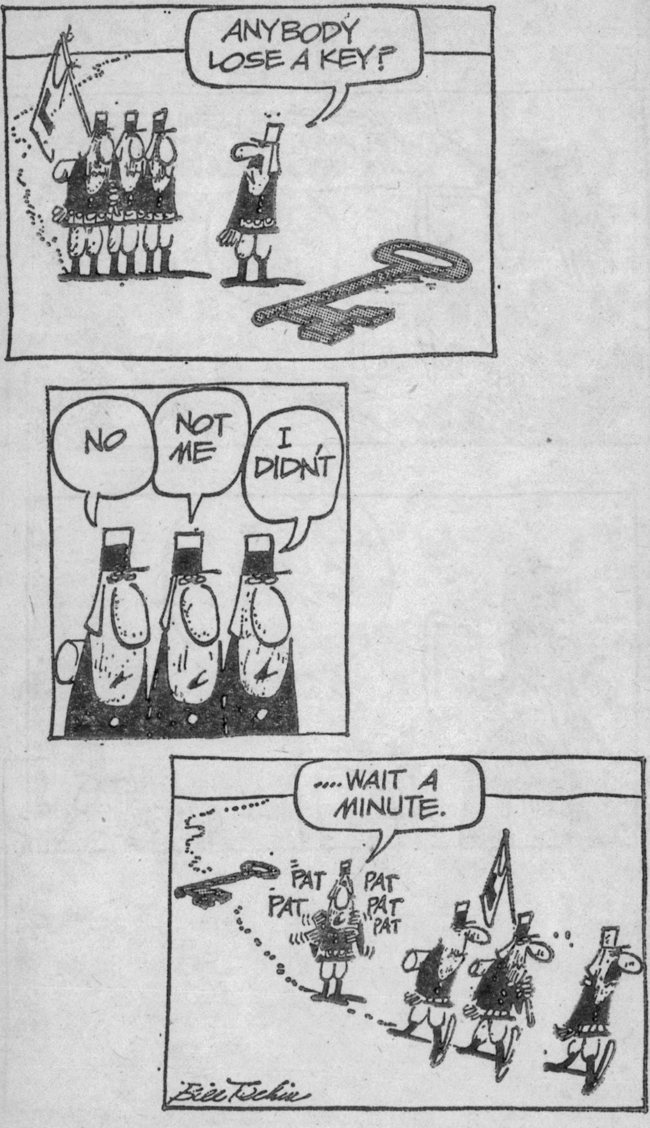
ANYBODY LOSE A KEY?
NO
NOT ME
I DIDN'T
....WAIT A MINUTE.
PAT PAT
PAT PAT PAT
PAT

friday

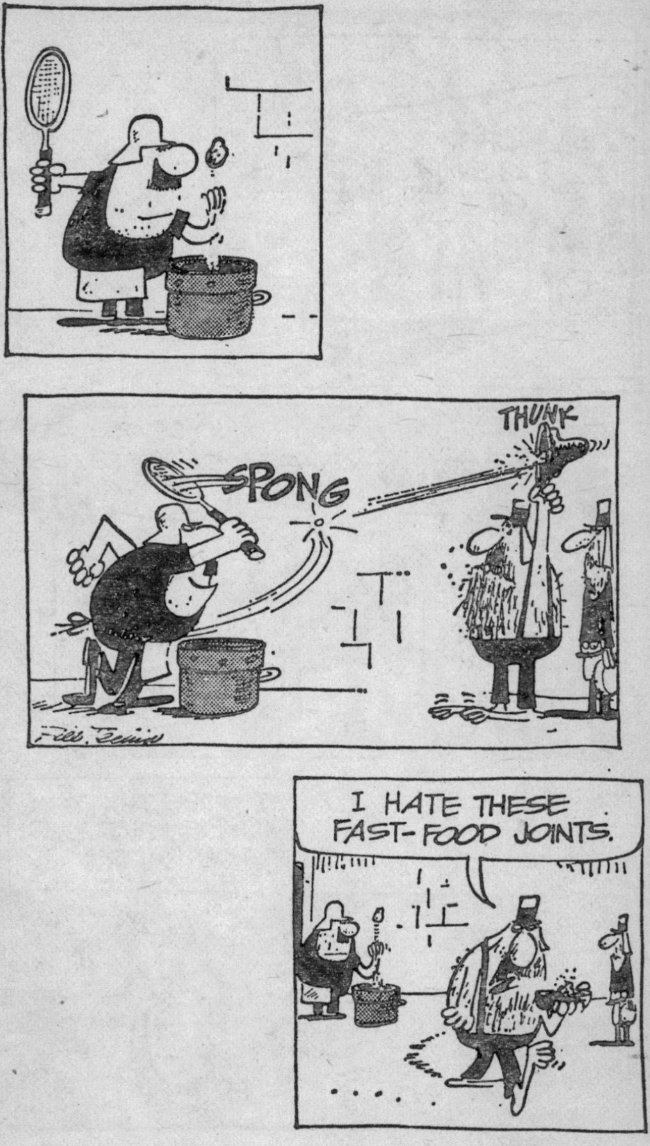
SPONG
THUNK
I HATE THESE FAST-FOOD JOINTS.

saturday

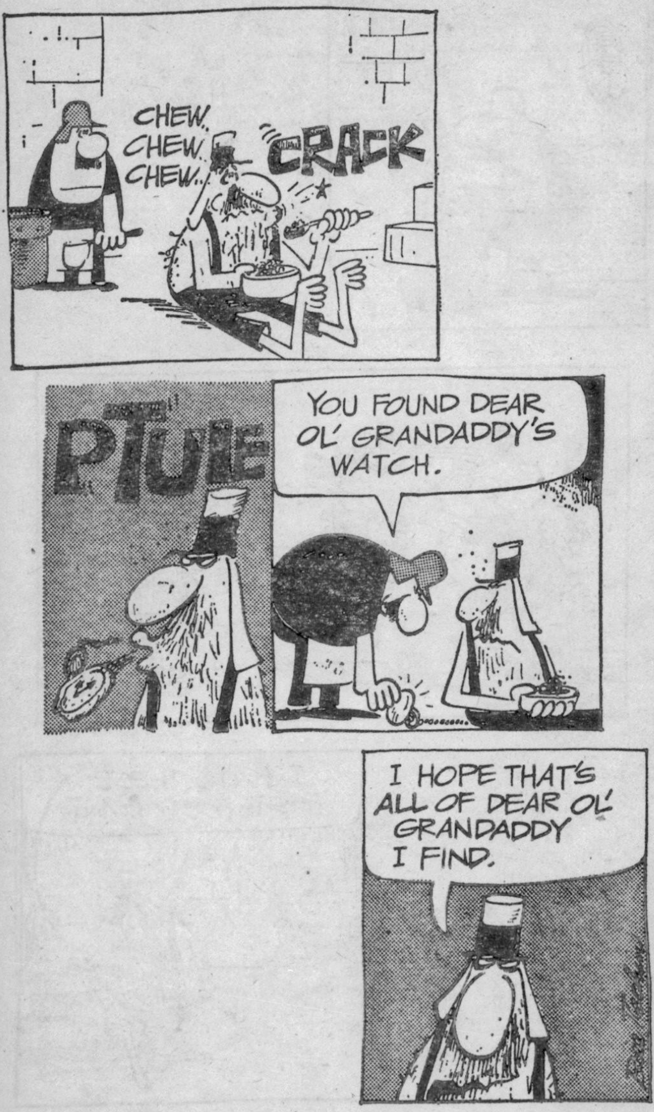
CHEW.
CHEW.
CHEW..
CRACK
PTUIE
YOU FOUND DEAR OL' GRANDADDY'S WATCH.
I HOPE THAT'S ALL OF DEAR OL' GRANDADDY I FIND.

monday

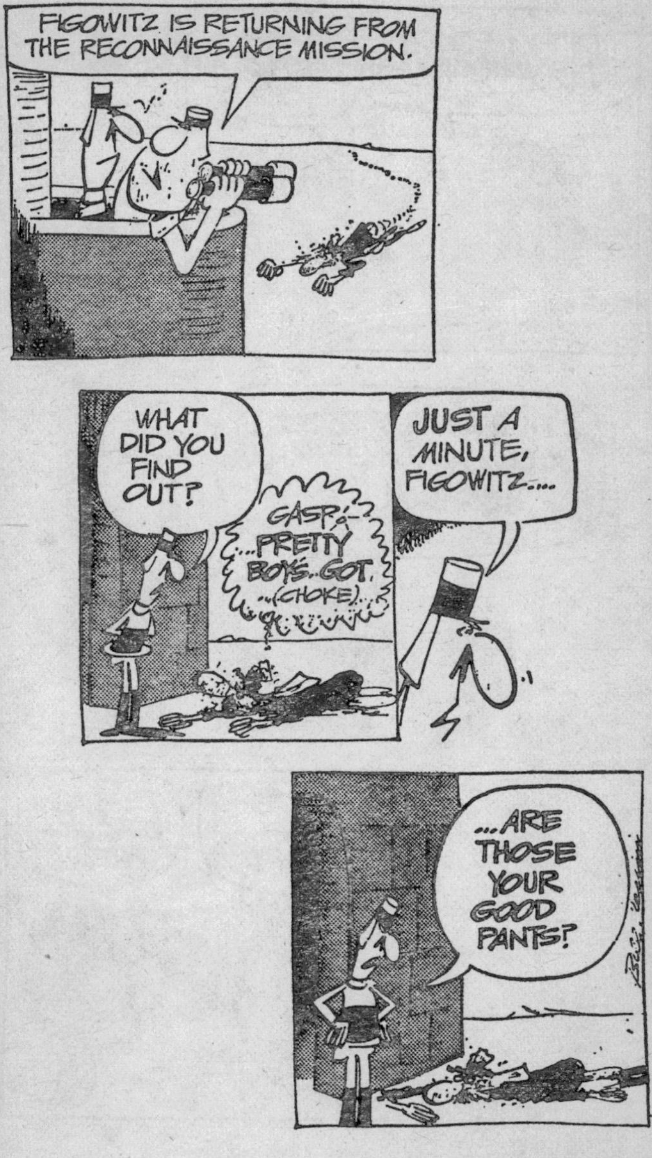
FIGOWITZ IS RETURNING FROM THE RECONNAISSANCE MISSION.
WHAT DID YOU FIND OUT?
GASP! ...PRETTY BOYS..GOT. ..(CHOKE)..
JUST A MINUTE, FIGOWITZ....
...ARE THOSE YOUR GOOD PANTS?

tuesday

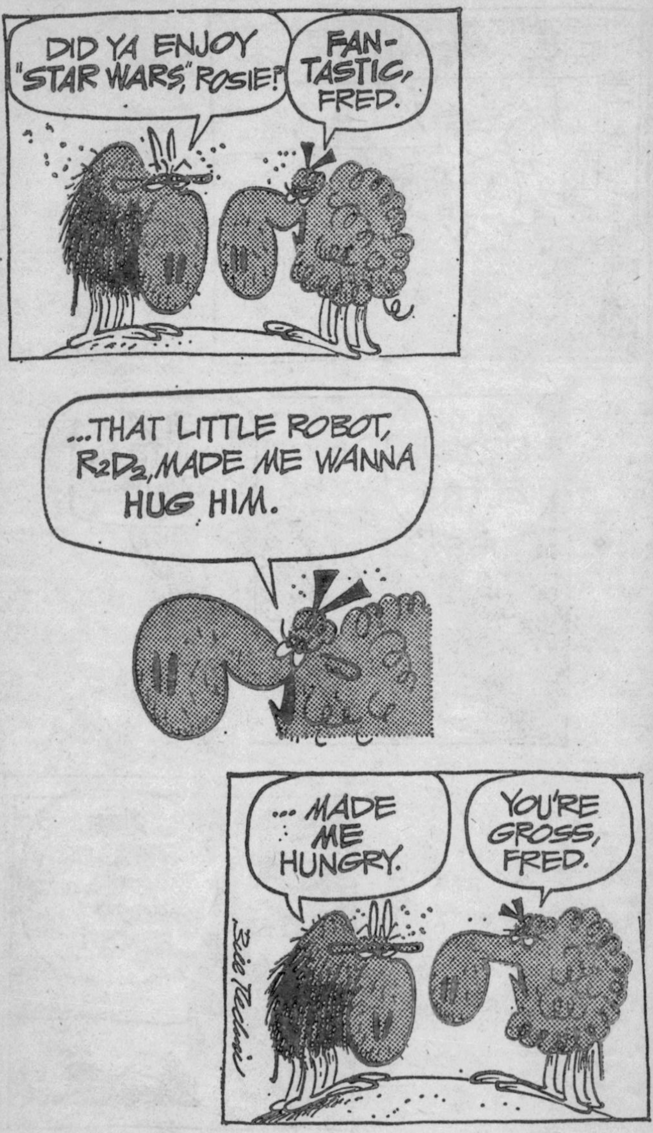
DID YA ENJOY "STAR WARS," ROSIE?
FAN-TASTIC, FRED.
...THAT LITTLE ROBOT, R2D2, MADE ME WANNA HUG HIM.
... MADE ME HUNGRY.
YOU'RE GROSS, FRED.

wednesday

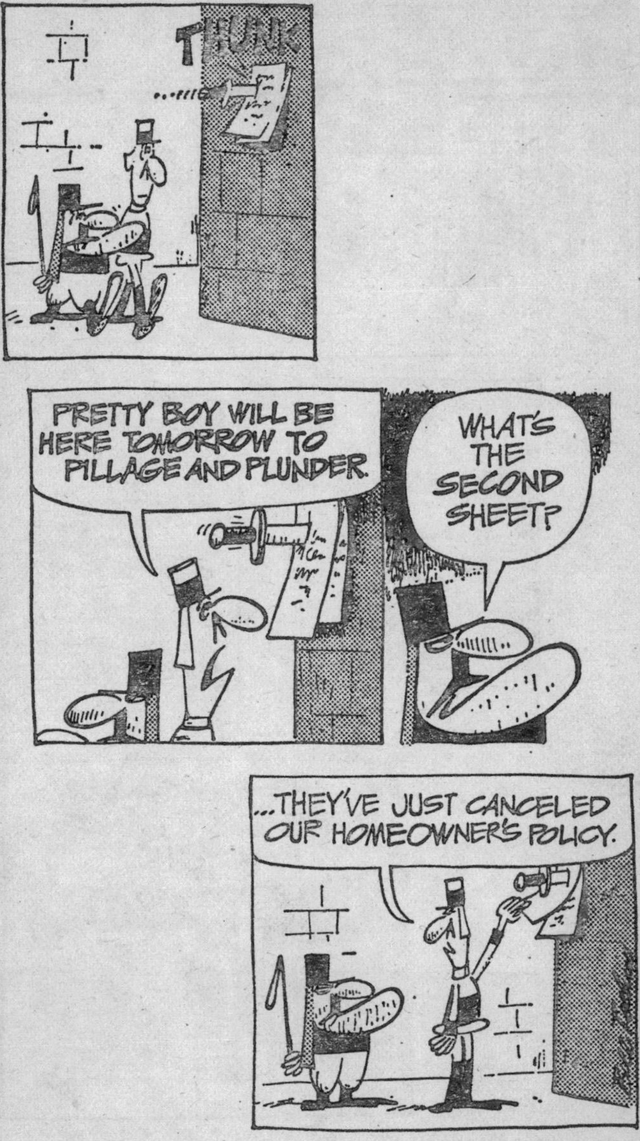
THUNK
PRETTY BOY WILL BE HERE TOMORROW TO PILLAGE AND PLUNDER.
WHAT'S THE SECOND SHEET?
...THEY'VE JUST CANCELED OUR HOMEOWNER'S POLICY.

thursday

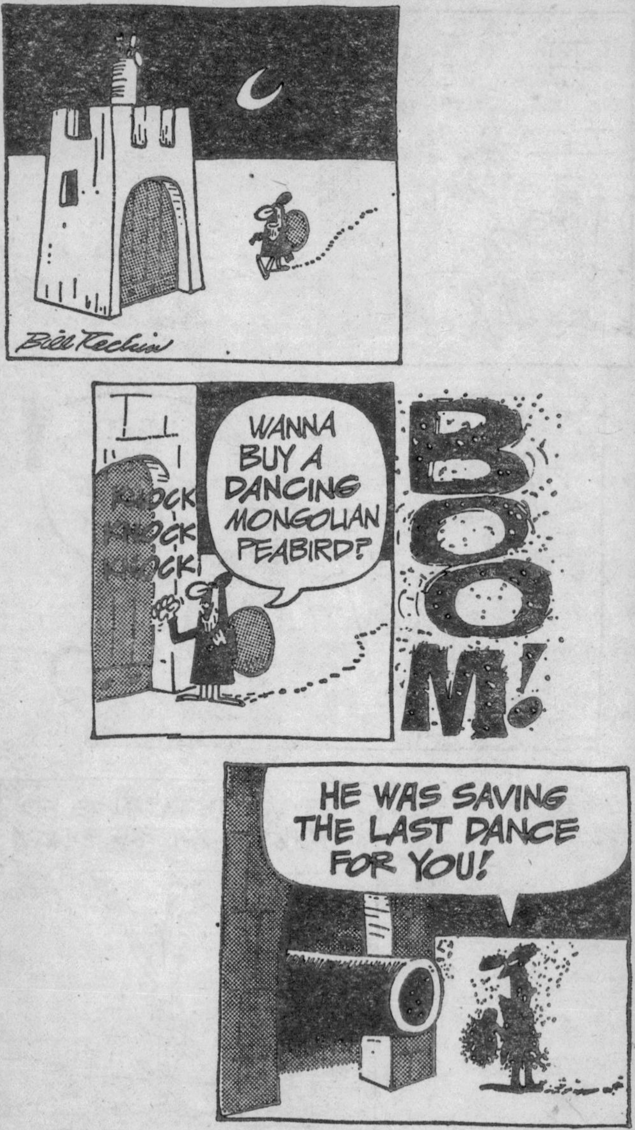
Bill Rechin
KNOCK
KNOCK
KNOCK
WANNA BUY A DANCING MONGOLIAN PEABIRD?
BOOM!
HE WAS SAVING THE LAST DANCE FOR YOU!

friday

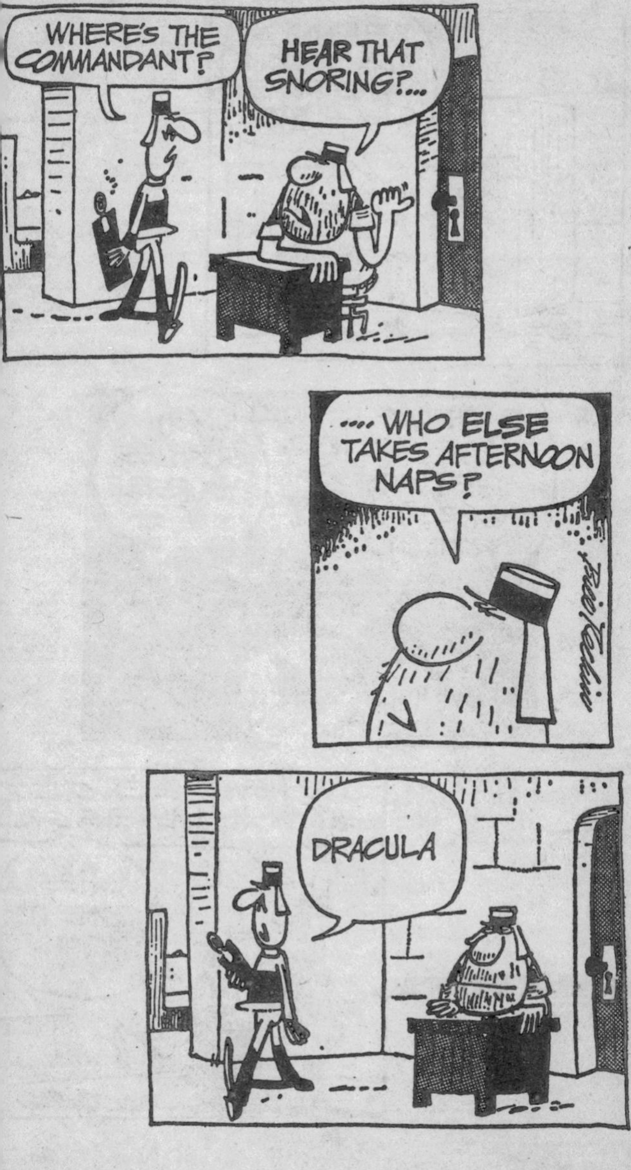
WHERE'S THE COMMANDANT?
HEAR THAT SNORING?...
....WHO ELSE TAKES AFTERNOON NAPS?
DRACULA

saturday

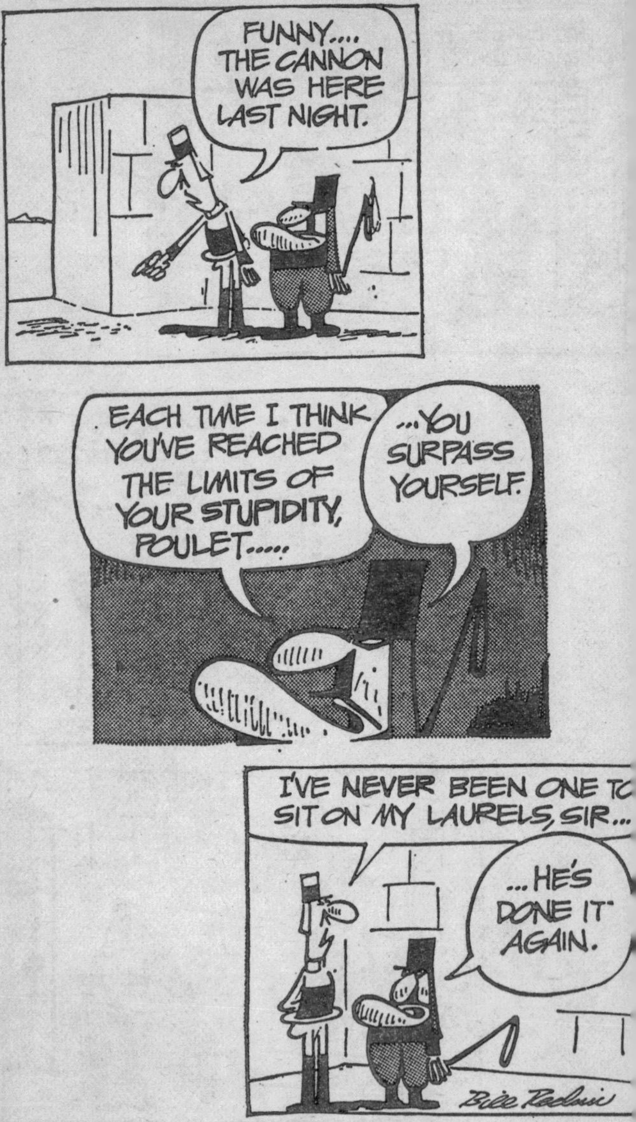
FUNNY.... THE CANNON WAS HERE LAST NIGHT.
EACH TIME I THINK YOU'VE REACHED THE LIMITS OF YOUR STUPIDITY, POULET.....
...YOU SURPASS YOURSELF.
I'VE NEVER BEEN ONE TO SIT ON MY LAURELS, SIR...
...HE'S DONE IT AGAIN.
Bill Radusic

monday

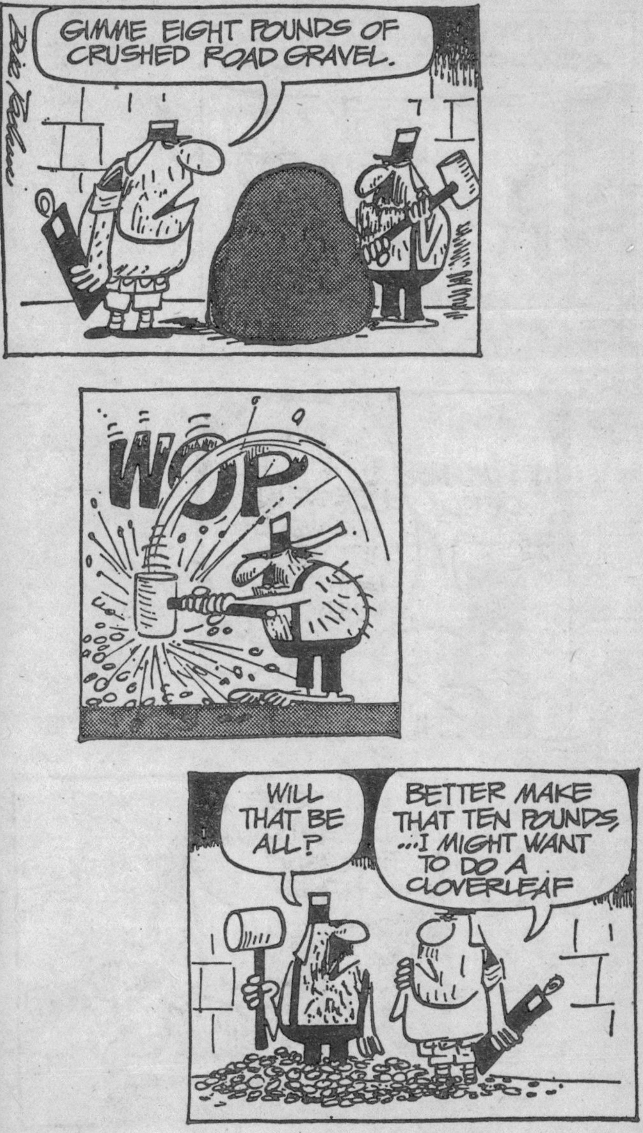
GIMME EIGHT POUNDS OF CRUSHED ROAD GRAVEL.
WOP
WILL THAT BE ALL?
BETTER MAKE THAT TEN POUNDS, ...I MIGHT WANT TO DO A CLOVERLEAF

tuesday

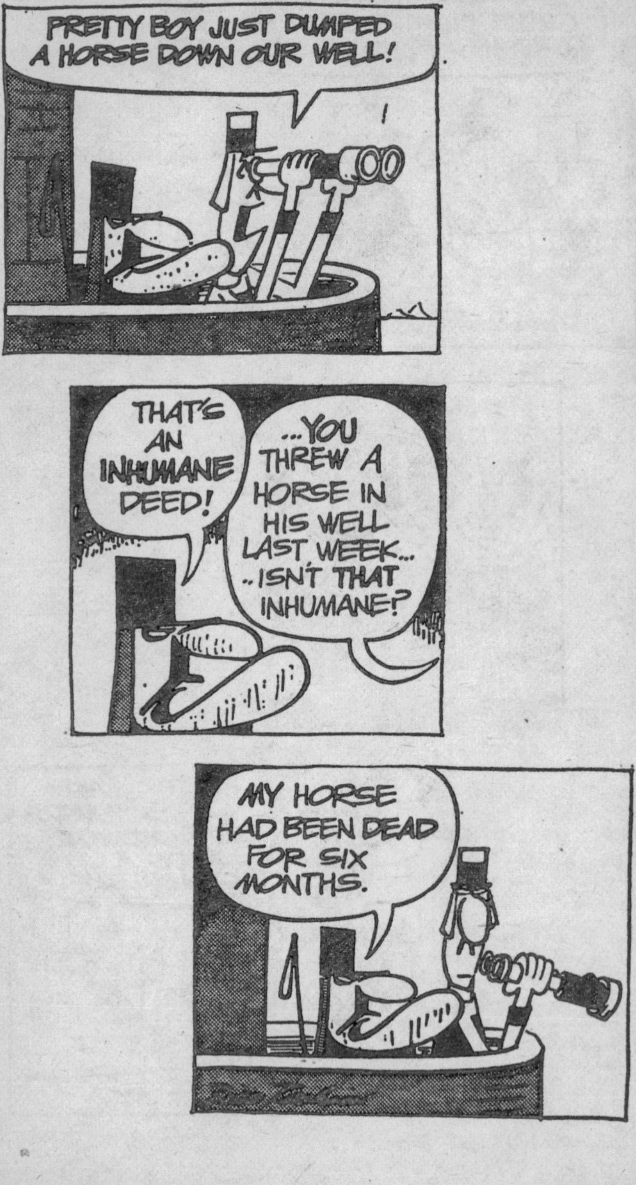
PRETTY BOY JUST DUMPED A HORSE DOWN OUR WELL!
THAT'S AN INHUMANE DEED!
...YOU THREW A HORSE IN HIS WELL LAST WEEK... ..ISN'T THAT INHUMANE?
MY HORSE HAD BEEN DEAD FOR SIX MONTHS.

wednesday

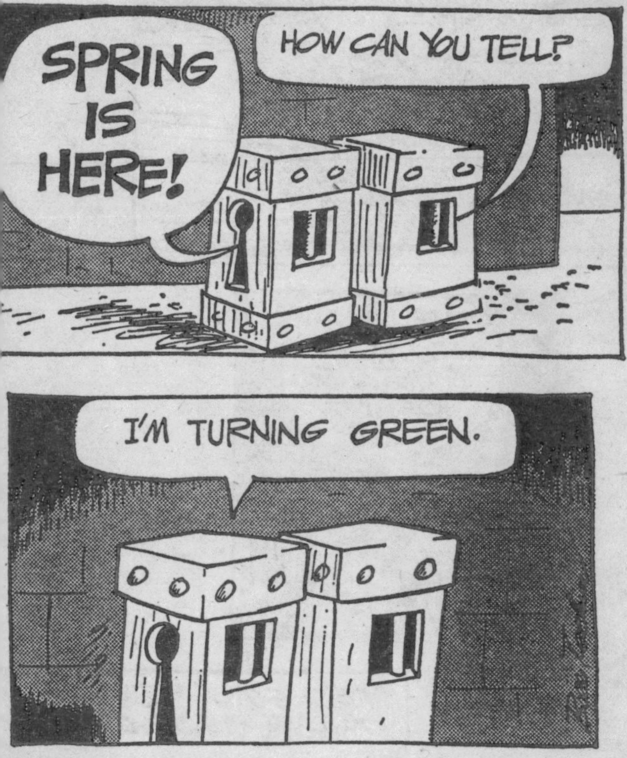
SPRING IS HERE!
HOW CAN YOU TELL?
I'M TURNING GREEN.

thursday

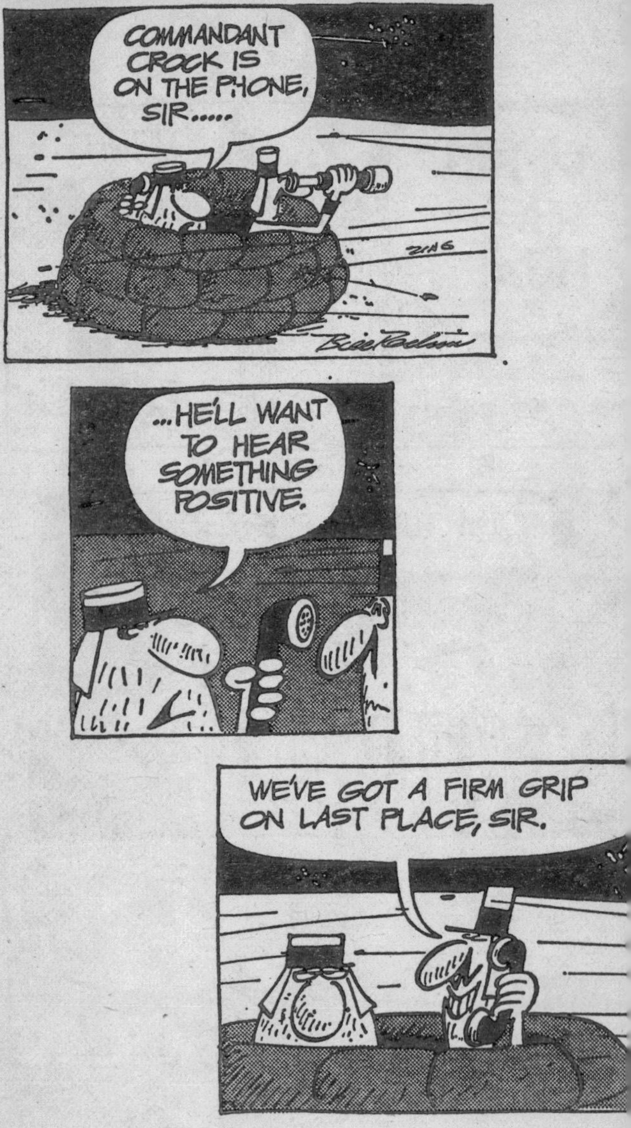
COMMANDANT CROCK IS ON THE PHONE, SIR.....
ZING
...HE'LL WANT TO HEAR SOMETHING POSITIVE.
WE'VE GOT A FIRM GRIP ON LAST PLACE, SIR.

friday

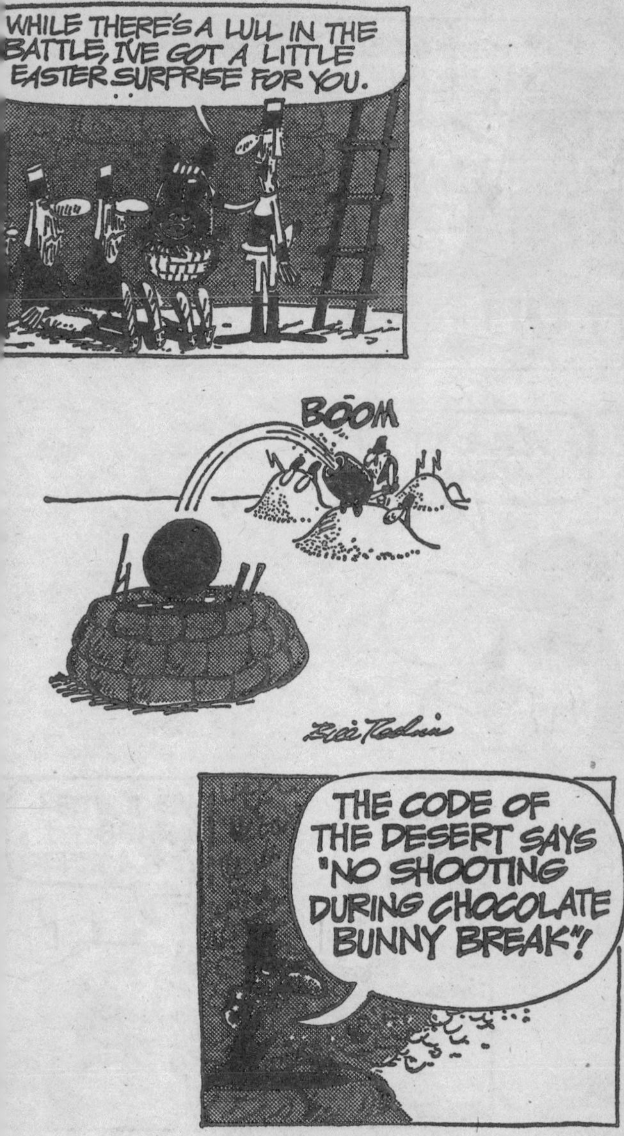
WHILE THERE'S A LULL IN THE BATTLE, I'VE GOT A LITTLE EASTER SURPRISE FOR YOU.
BOOM
THE CODE OF THE DESERT SAYS "NO SHOOTING DURING CHOCOLATE BUNNY BREAK"!

saturday

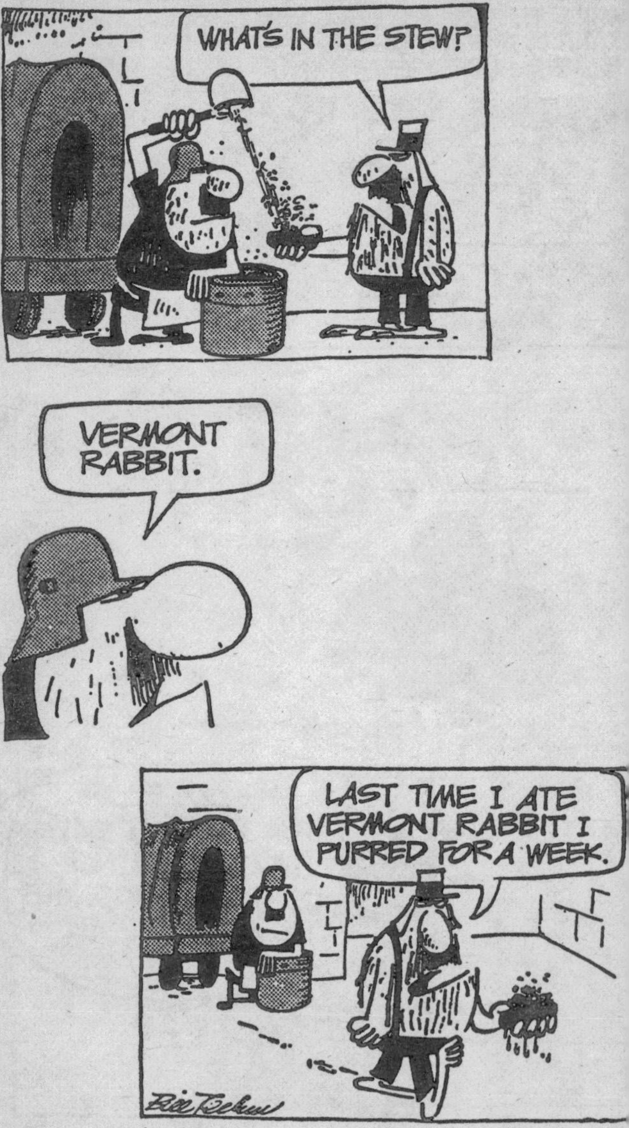
WHAT'S IN THE STEW?
VERMONT RABBIT.
LAST TIME I ATE VERMONT RABBIT I PURRED FOR A WEEK.

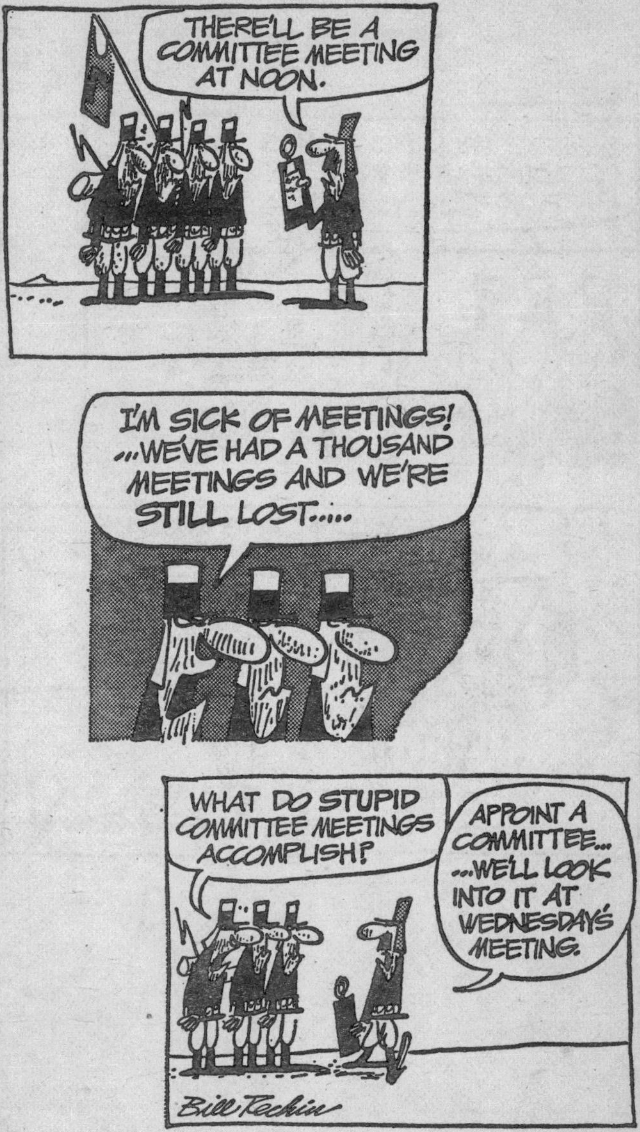
THERE'LL BE A COMMITTEE MEETING AT NOON.
I'M SICK OF MEETINGS! ...WE'VE HAD A THOUSAND MEETINGS AND WE'RE STILL LOST.....
WHAT DO STUPID COMMITTEE MEETINGS ACCOMPLISH?
APPOINT A COMMITTEE... ...WE'LL LOOK INTO IT AT WEDNESDAY'S MEETING.
Bill Rechin

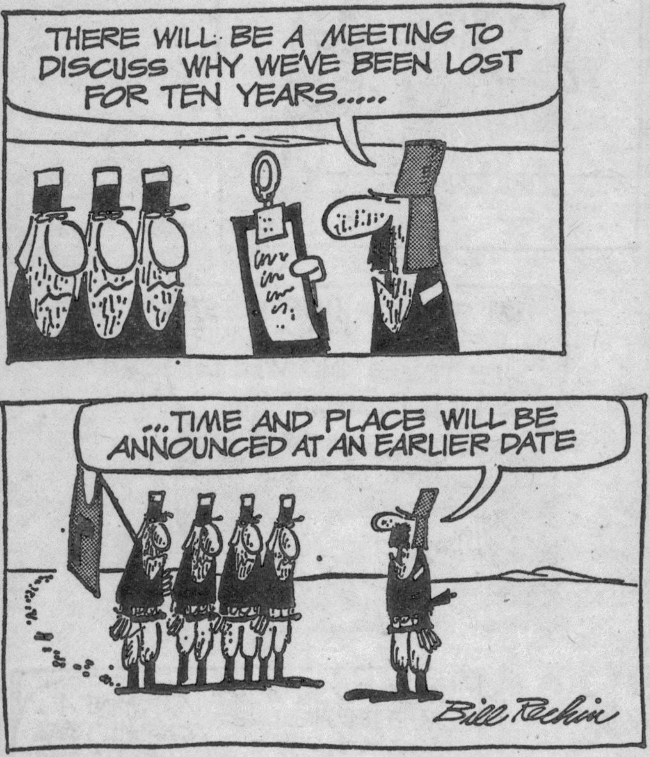
THERE WILL BE A MEETING TO DISCUSS WHY WE'VE BEEN LOST FOR TEN YEARS.....
...TIME AND PLACE WILL BE ANNOUNCED AT AN EARLIER DATE
Bill Rechin

wednesday

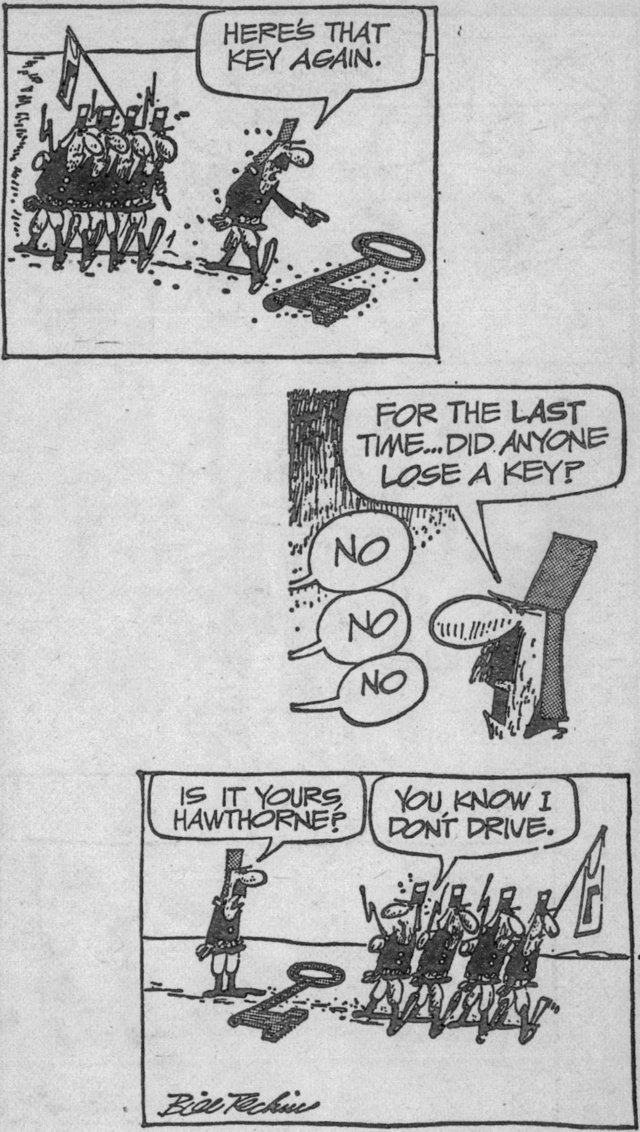
HERE'S THAT KEY AGAIN.
FOR THE LAST TIME...DID ANYONE LOSE A KEY?
NO
NO
NO
IS IT YOURS, HAWTHORNE?
YOU KNOW I DON'T DRIVE.
Bill Rechin

thursday

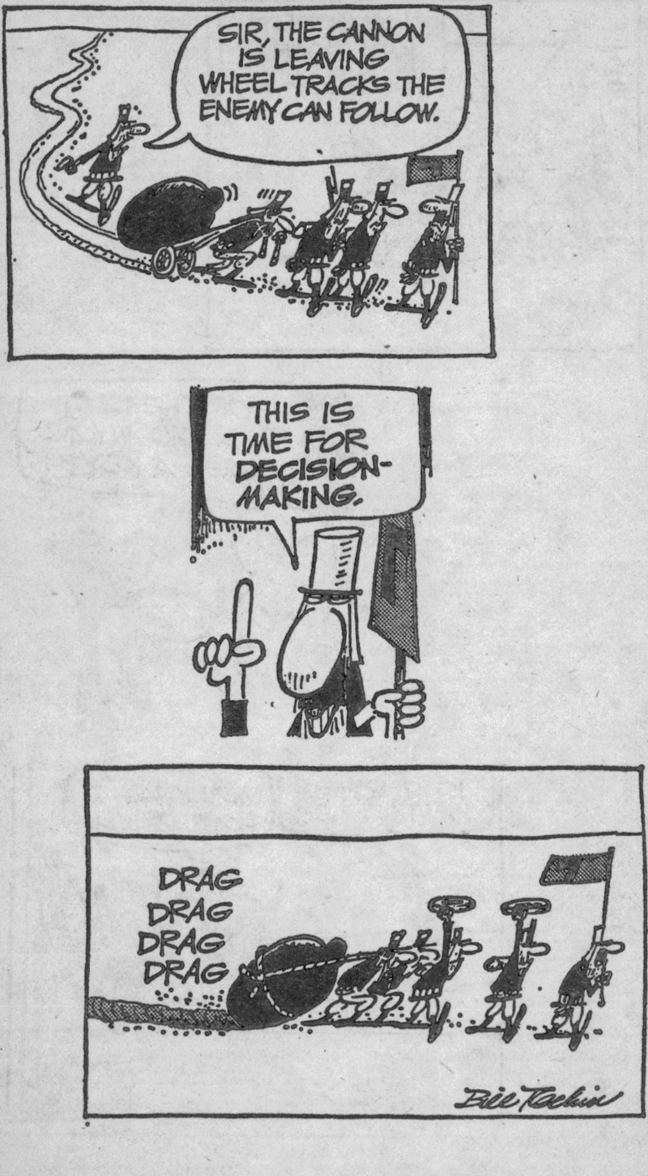
SIR, THE CANNON IS LEAVING WHEEL TRACKS THE ENEMY CAN FOLLOW.
THIS IS TIME FOR DECISION-MAKING.
DRAG DRAG DRAG DRAG
Bill Rechin

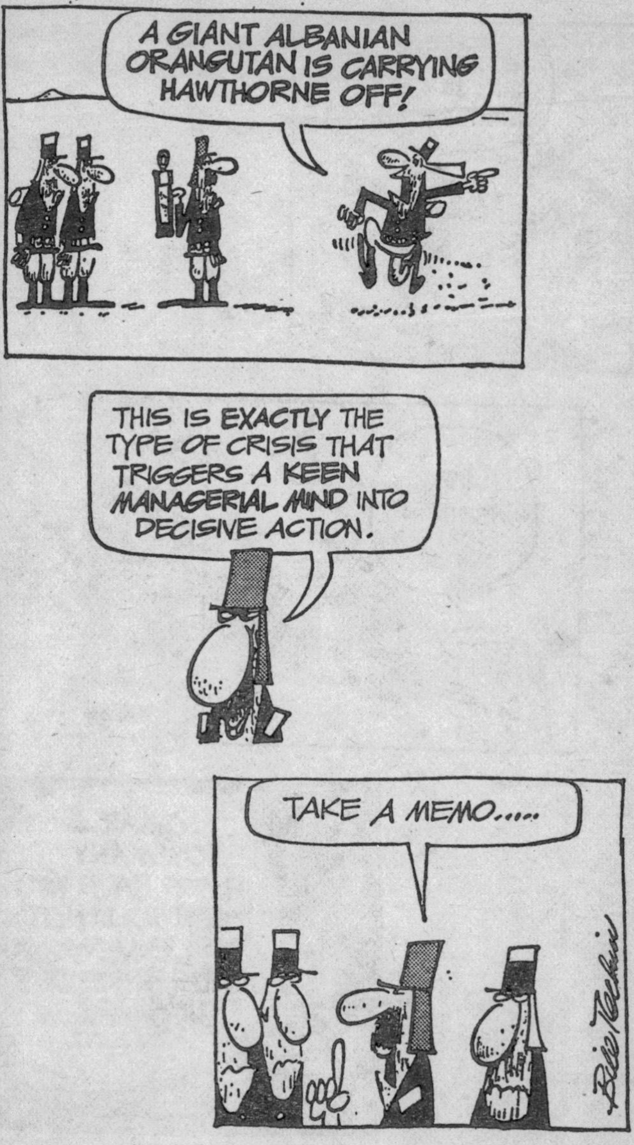
A GIANT ALBANIAN ORANGUTAN IS CARRYING HAWTHORNE OFF!
THIS IS EXACTLY THE TYPE OF CRISIS THAT TRIGGERS A KEEN MANAGERIAL MIND INTO DECISIVE ACTION.
TAKE A MEMO.....

saturday

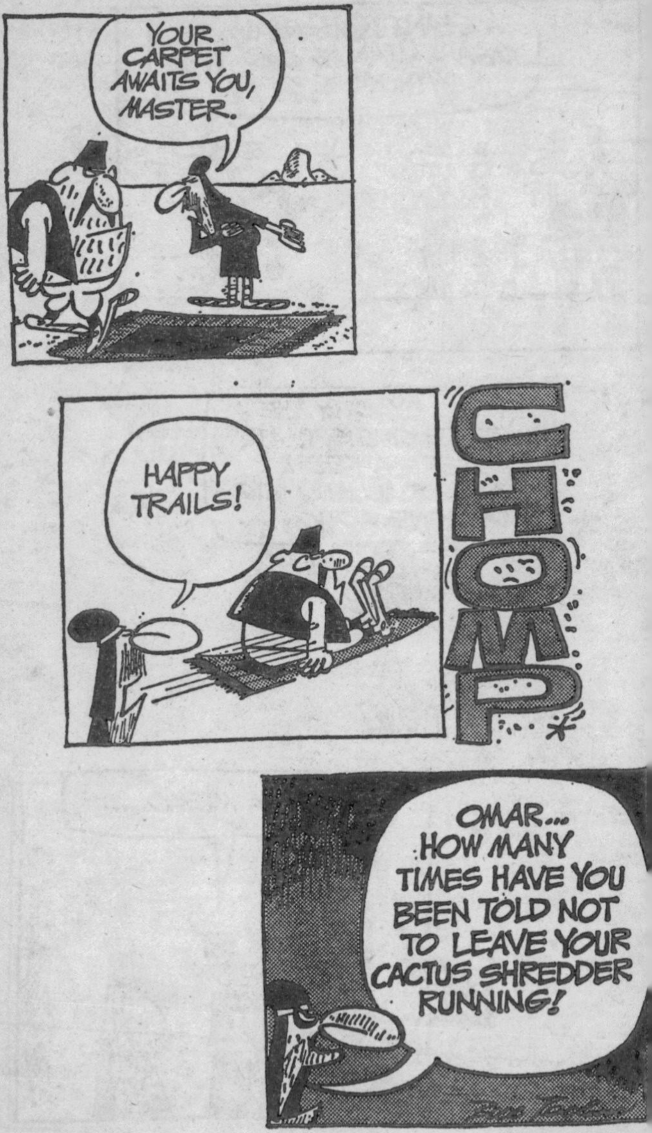
YOUR CARPET AWAITS YOU, MASTER.
HAPPY TRAILS!
CHOMP
OMAR... HOW MANY TIMES HAVE YOU BEEN TOLD NOT TO LEAVE YOUR CACTUS SHREDDER RUNNING!

monday

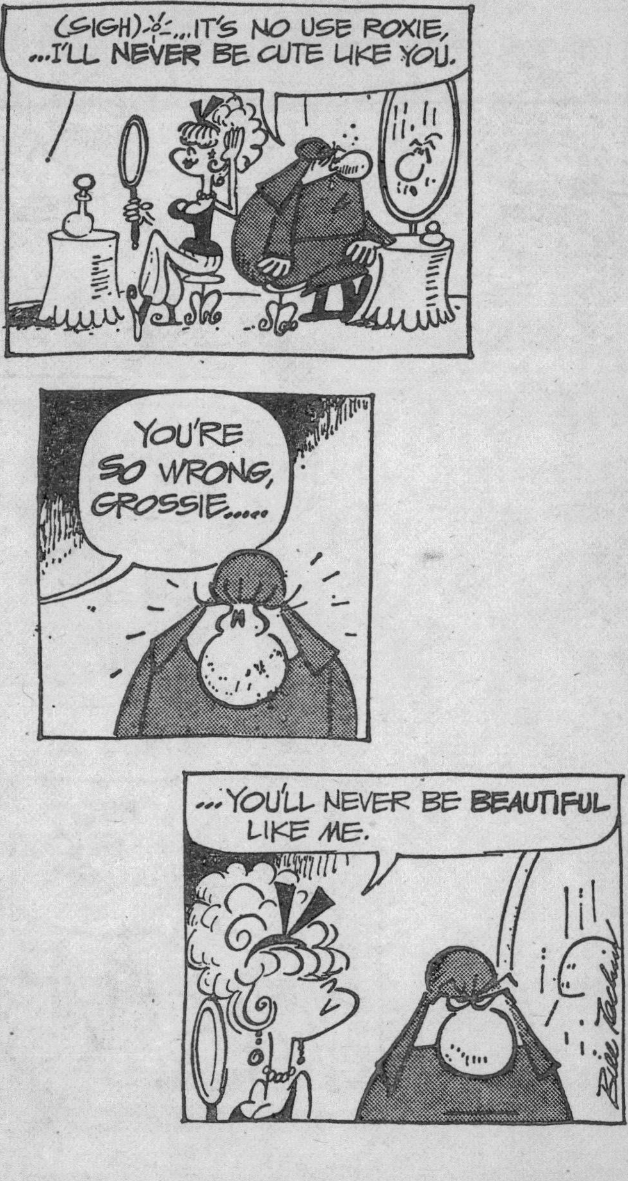
(SIGH) ...IT'S NO USE ROXIE, ...I'LL NEVER BE CUTE LIKE YOU.
YOU'RE SO WRONG, GROSSIE.....
...YOU'LL NEVER BE BEAUTIFUL LIKE ME.

tuesday

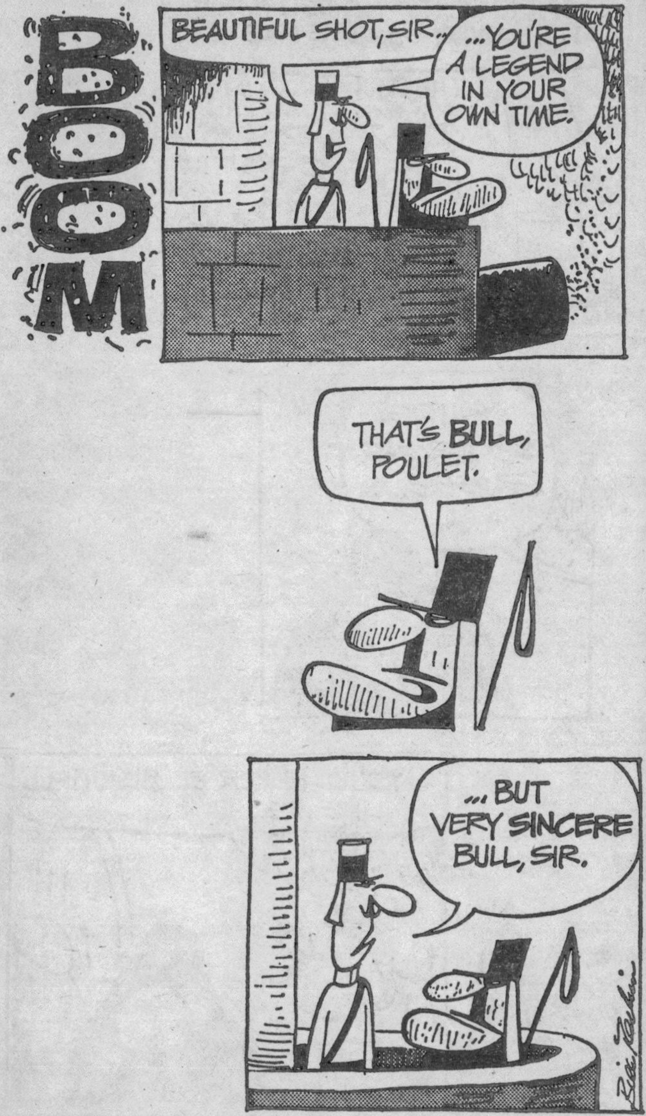
BOOM
BEAUTIFUL SHOT, SIR...
...YOU'RE A LEGEND IN YOUR OWN TIME.
THAT'S BULL, POULET.
...BUT VERY SINCERE BULL, SIR.

wednesday

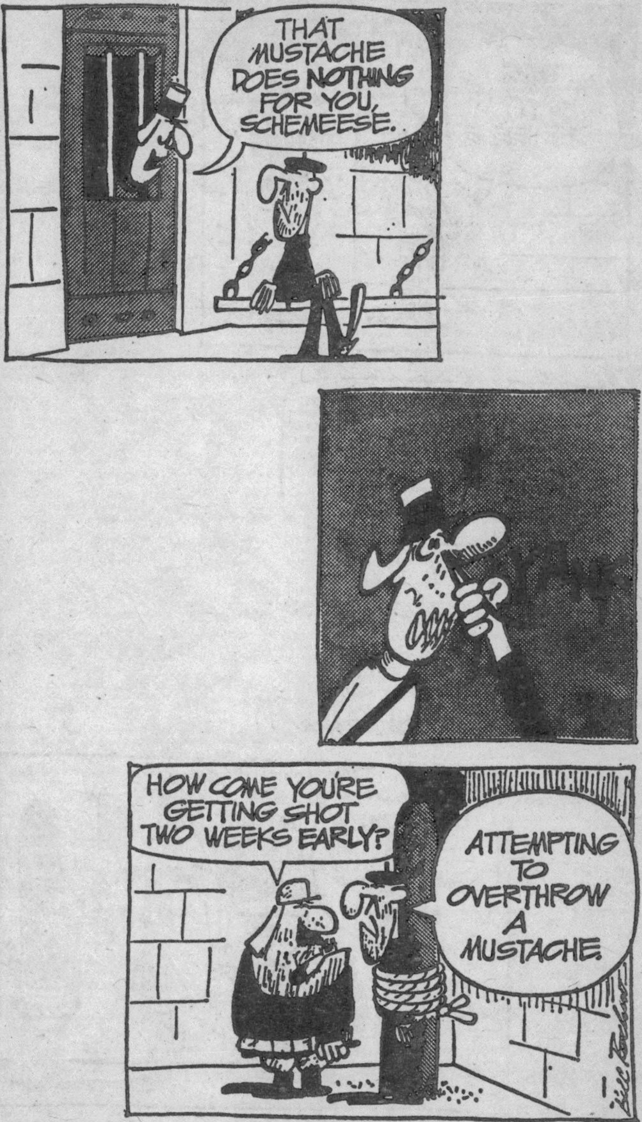
THAT MUSTACHE DOES NOTHING FOR YOU, SCHEMEESE.
HOW COME YOU'RE GETTING SHOT TWO WEEKS EARLY?
ATTEMPTING TO OVERTHROW A MUSTACHE.

thursday

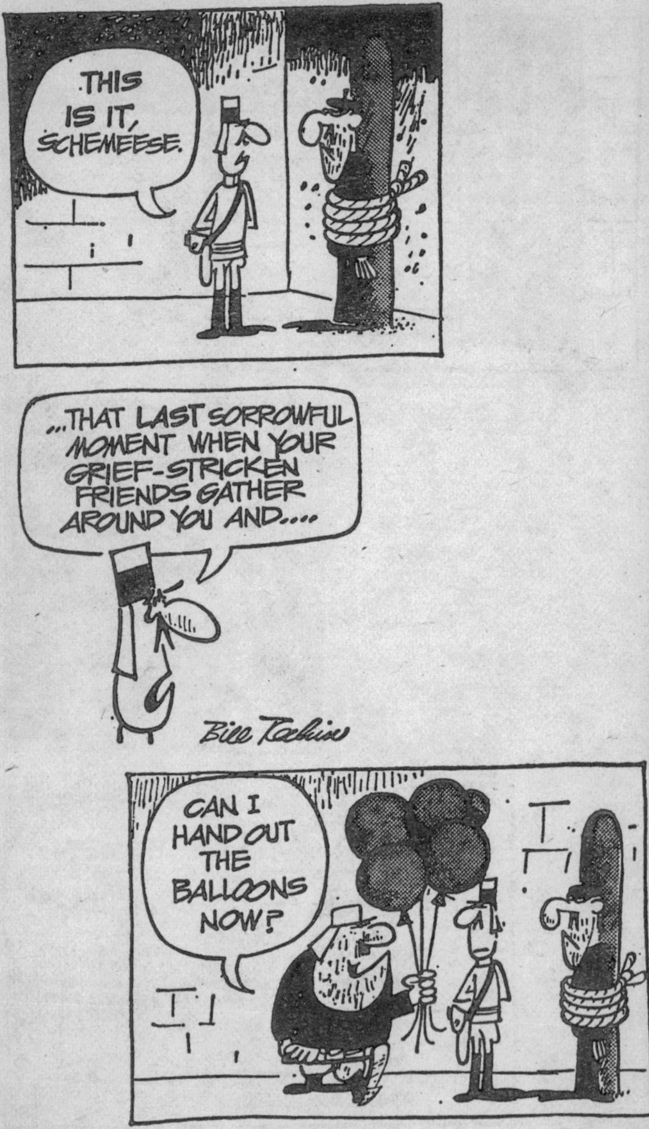
THIS IS IT, SCHEMEESE.
...THAT LAST SORROWFUL MOMENT WHEN YOUR GRIEF-STRICKEN FRIENDS GATHER AROUND YOU AND....
Bill Rechin
CAN I HAND OUT THE BALLOONS NOW?

friday

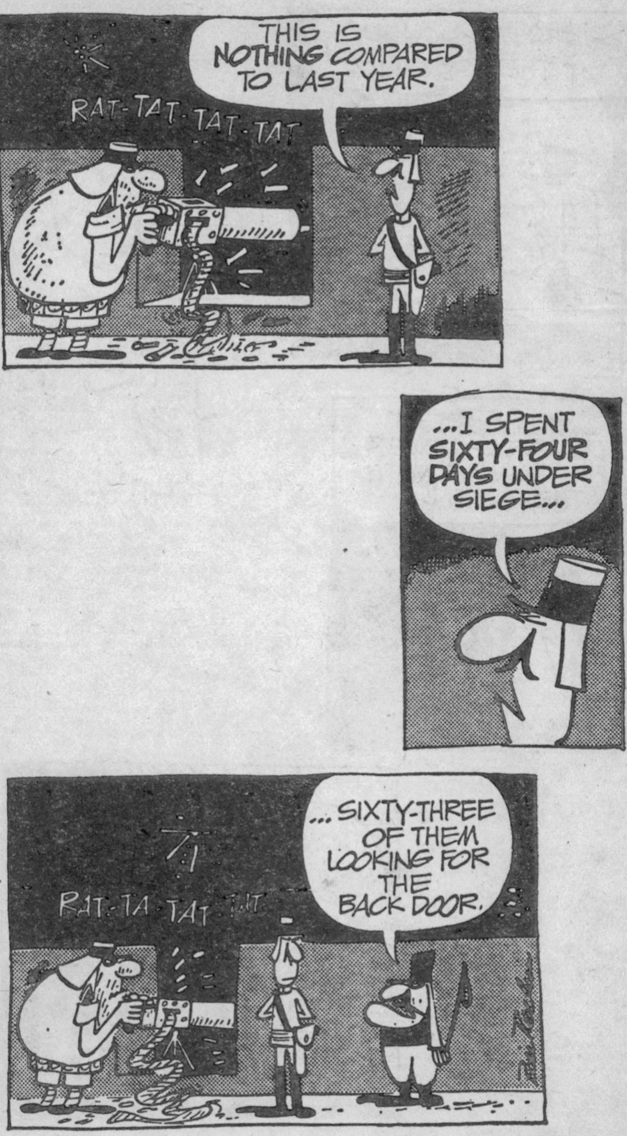

THIS IS NOTHING COMPARED TO LAST YEAR.
RAT-TAT-TAT-TAT
...I SPENT SIXTY-FOUR DAYS UNDER SIEGE...
...SIXTY-THREE OF THEM LOOKING FOR THE BACK DOOR.
RAT-TA-TAT

saturday

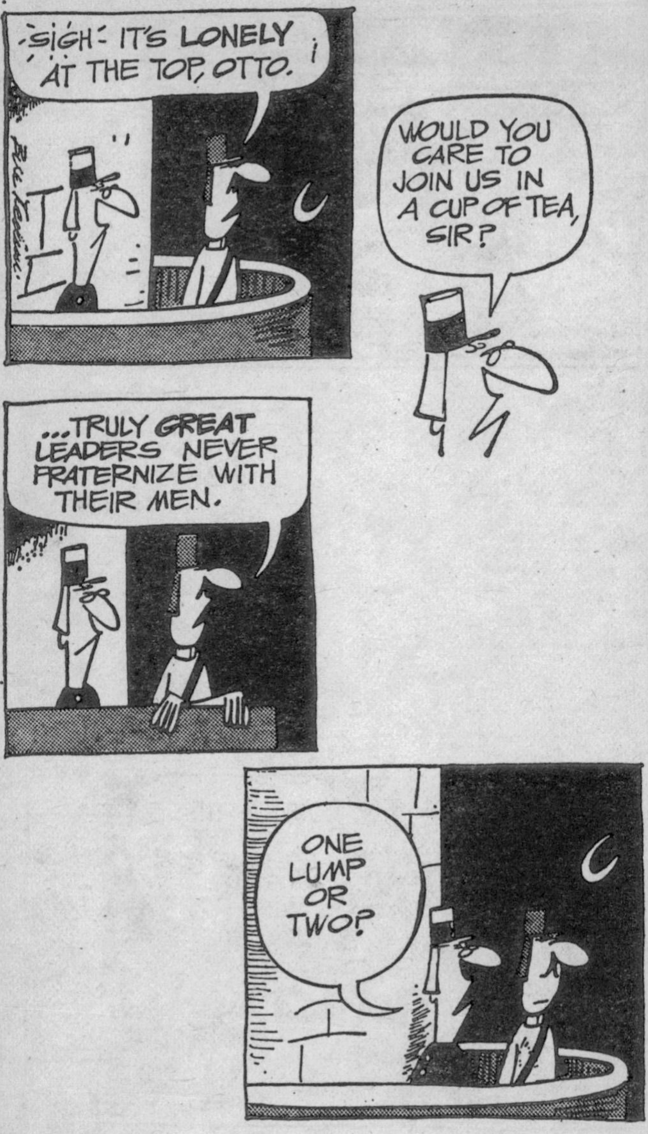

-SIGH- IT'S LONELY AT THE TOP, OTTO.
WOULD YOU CARE TO JOIN US IN A CUP OF TEA, SIR?
...TRULY GREAT LEADERS NEVER FRATERNIZE WITH THEIR MEN.
ONE LUMP OR TWO?

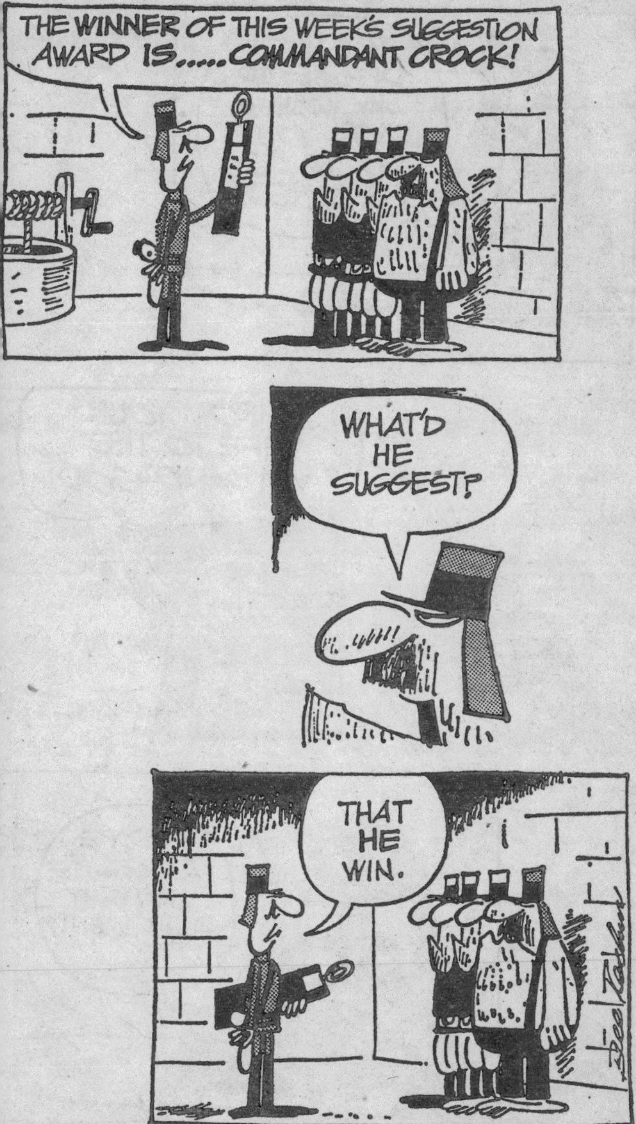
THE WINNER OF THIS WEEK'S SUGGESTION AWARD IS.....COMMANDANT CROCK!
WHAT'D HE SUGGEST?
THAT HE WIN.

tuesday

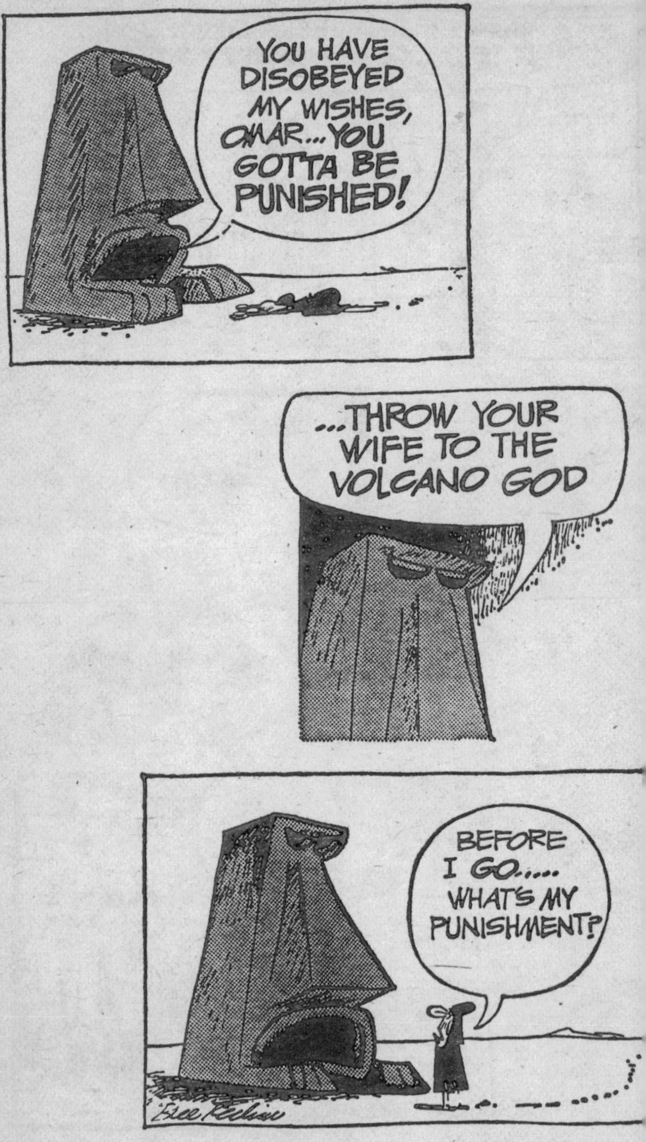
YOU HAVE DISOBEYED MY WISHES, OMAR... YOU GOTTA BE PUNISHED!
...THROW YOUR WIFE TO THE VOLCANO GOD
BEFORE I GO..... WHAT'S MY PUNISHMENT?

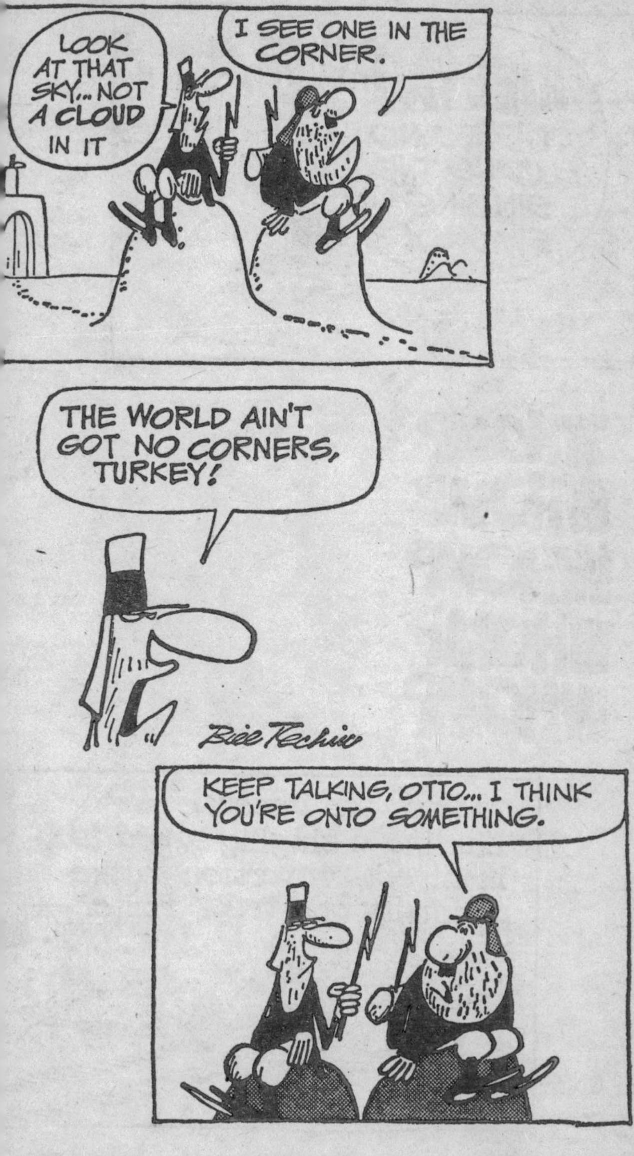
LOOK AT THAT SKY... NOT A CLOUD IN IT
I SEE ONE IN THE CORNER.
THE WORLD AIN'T GOT NO CORNERS, TURKEY!
Bill Rechin
KEEP TALKING, OTTO... I THINK YOU'RE ONTO SOMETHING.

thursday

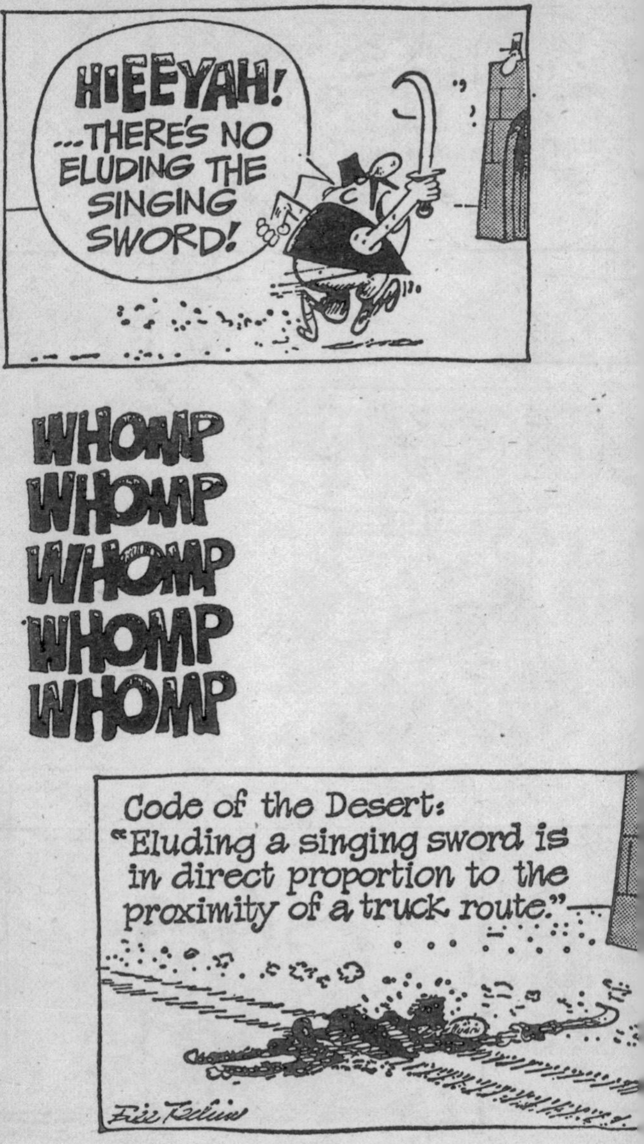
HIEEEYAH! ...THERE'S NO ELUDING THE SINGING SWORD!
WHOMP
WHOMP
WHOMP
WHOMP
WHOMP
Code of the Desert:
"Eluding a singing sword is in direct proportion to the proximity of a truck route."

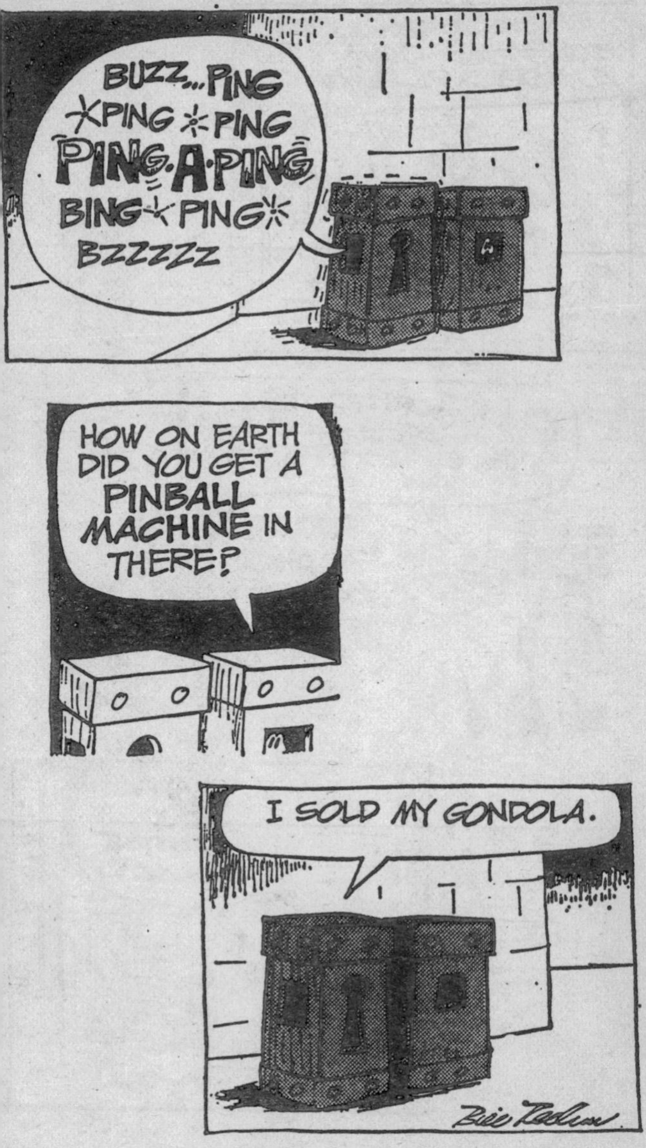
BUZZ... PING PING PING PING-A-PING BING PING BZZZZZ
HOW ON EARTH DID YOU GET A PINBALL MACHINE IN THERE?
I SOLD MY GONDOLA.

saturday

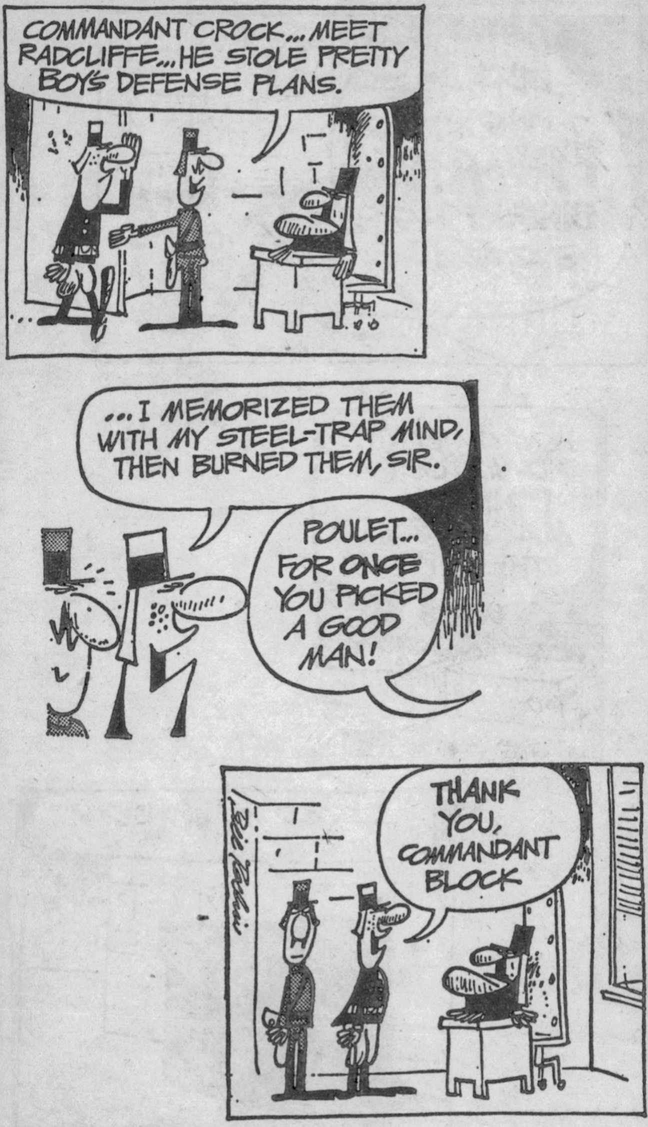
COMMANDANT CROCK... MEET RADCLIFFE... HE STOLE PRETTY BOY'S DEFENSE PLANS.
...I MEMORIZED THEM WITH MY STEEL-TRAP MIND, THEN BURNED THEM, SIR.
POULET... FOR ONCE YOU PICKED A GOOD MAN!
THANK YOU, COMMANDANT BLOCK

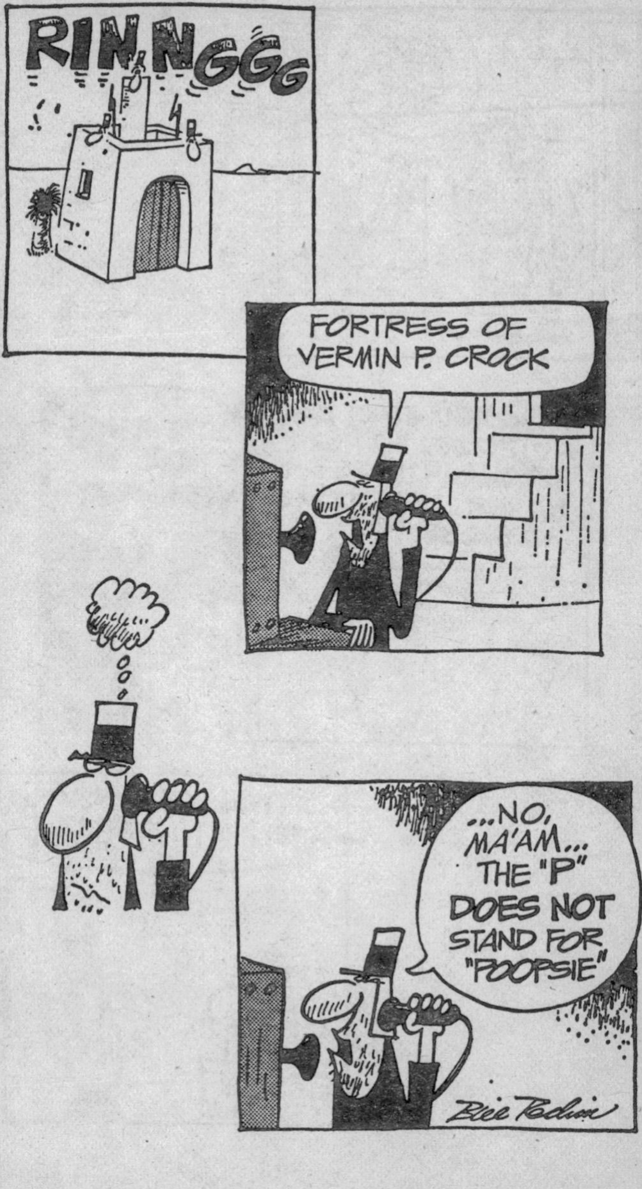
RINNGGG
FORTRESS OF VERMIN P. CROCK
...NO, MA'AM... THE "P" DOES NOT STAND FOR "POOPSIE"
Bill Rechin

tuesday

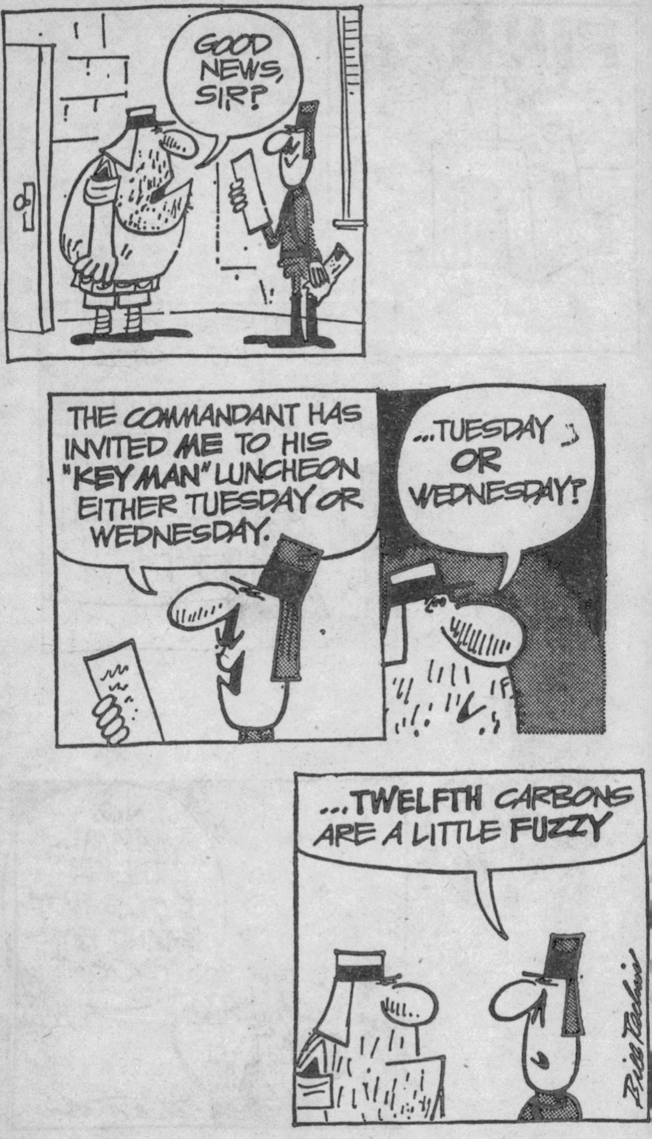
GOOD NEWS, SIR?
THE COMMANDANT HAS INVITED ME TO HIS "KEY MAN" LUNCHEON EITHER TUESDAY OR WEDNESDAY.
...TUESDAY OR WEDNESDAY?
...TWELFTH CARBONS ARE A LITTLE FUZZY
Bill Rechin

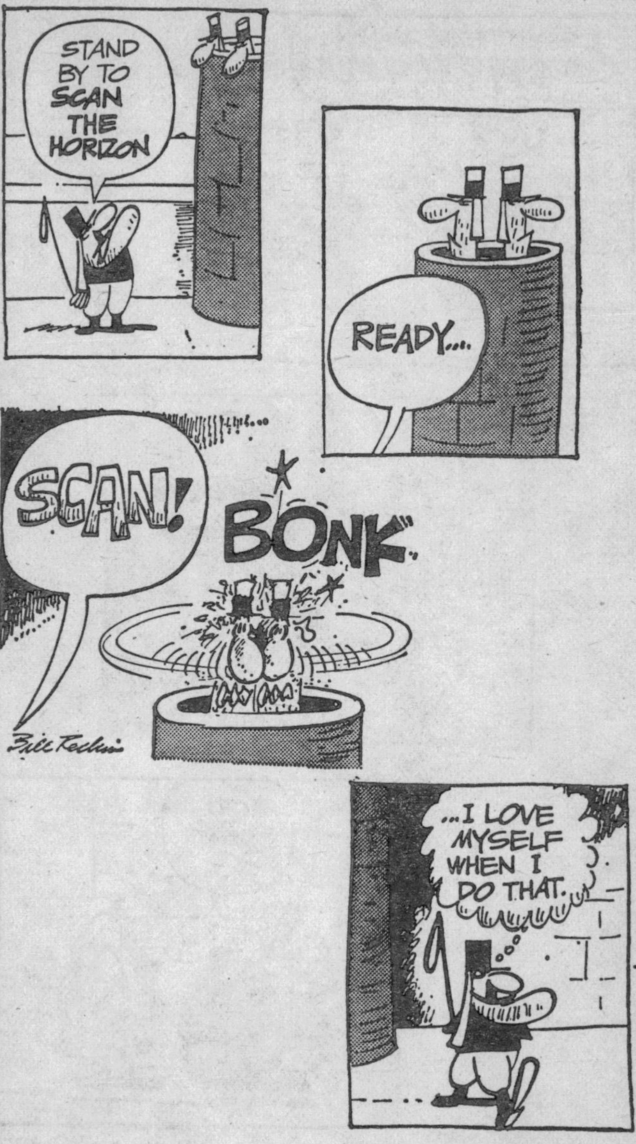
STAND BY TO SCAN THE HORIZON
READY....
SCAN!
BONK
...I LOVE MYSELF WHEN I DO THAT.
Bill Rechin

thursday

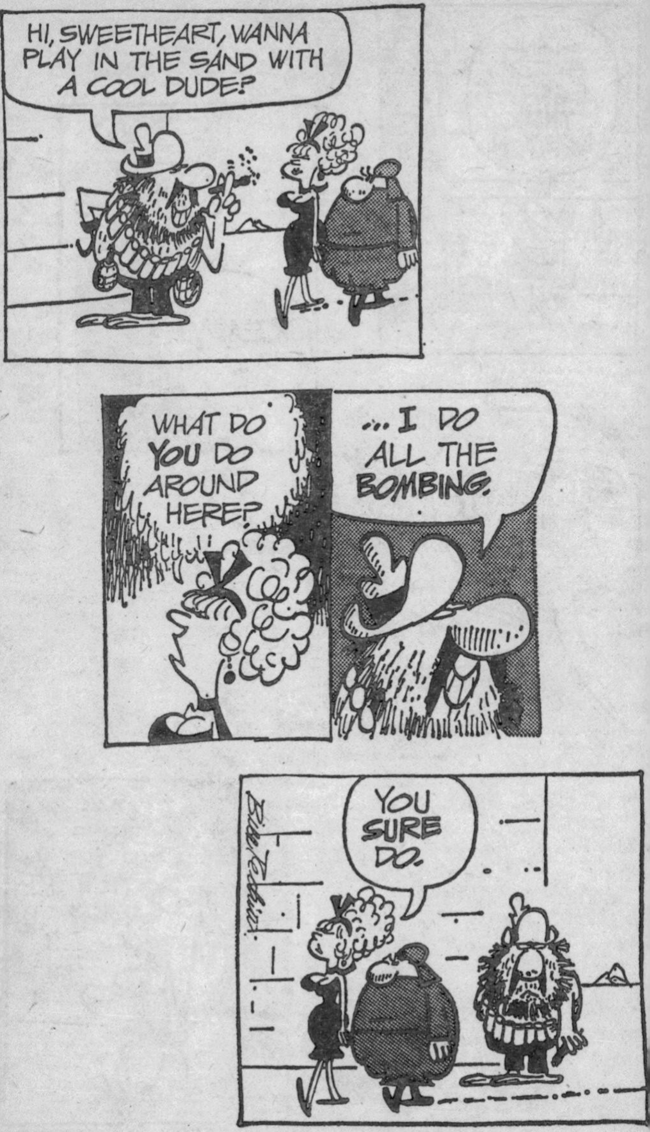
HI, SWEETHEART, WANNA PLAY IN THE SAND WITH A COOL DUDE?
WHAT DO YOU DO AROUND HERE?
...I DO ALL THE BOMBING.
YOU SURE DO.

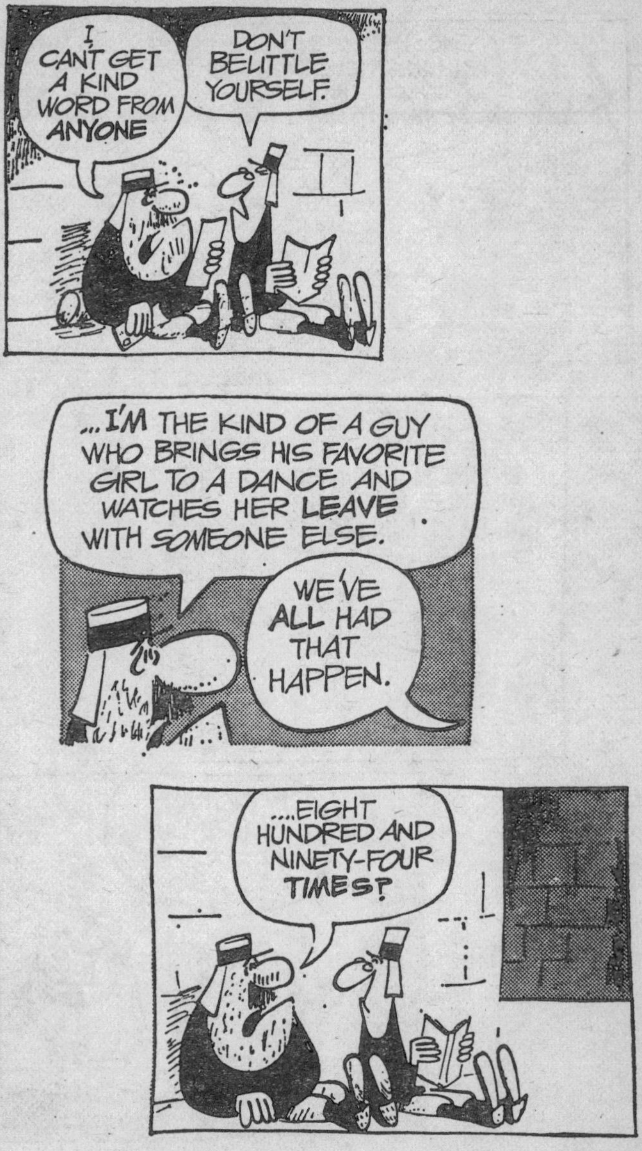
I CAN'T GET A KIND WORD FROM ANYONE
DON'T BELITTLE YOURSELF.
...I'M THE KIND OF A GUY WHO BRINGS HIS FAVORITE GIRL TO A DANCE AND WATCHES HER LEAVE WITH SOMEONE ELSE.
WE'VE ALL HAD THAT HAPPEN.
....EIGHT HUNDRED AND NINETY-FOUR TIMES?

saturday

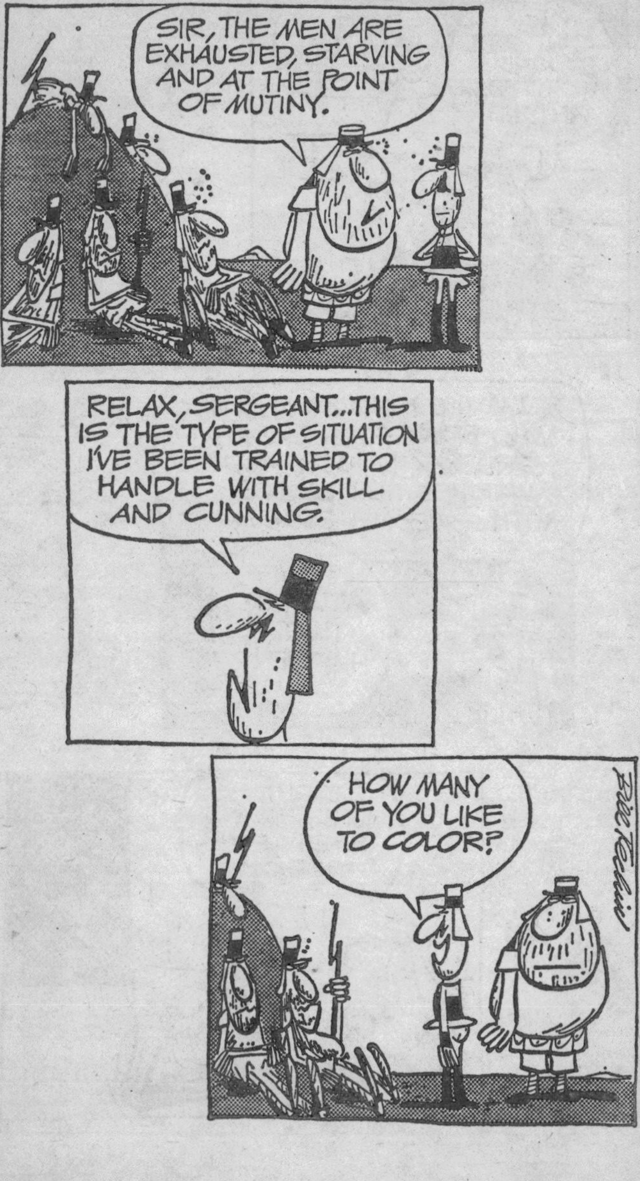
SIR, THE MEN ARE EXHAUSTED, STARVING AND AT THE POINT OF MUTINY.
RELAX, SERGEANT...THIS IS THE TYPE OF SITUATION I'VE BEEN TRAINED TO HANDLE WITH SKILL AND CUNNING.
HOW MANY OF YOU LIKE TO COLOR?

monday

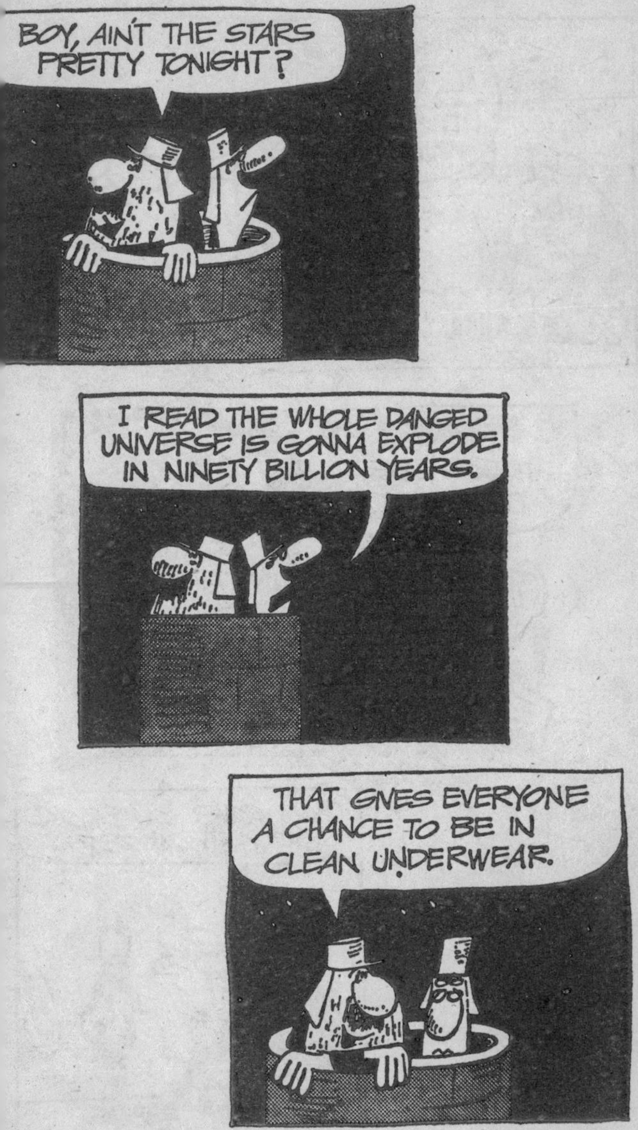
BOY, AIN'T THE STARS PRETTY TONIGHT?
I READ THE WHOLE DANGED UNIVERSE IS GONNA EXPLODE IN NINETY BILLION YEARS.
THAT GIVES EVERYONE A CHANCE TO BE IN CLEAN UNDERWEAR.

tuesday

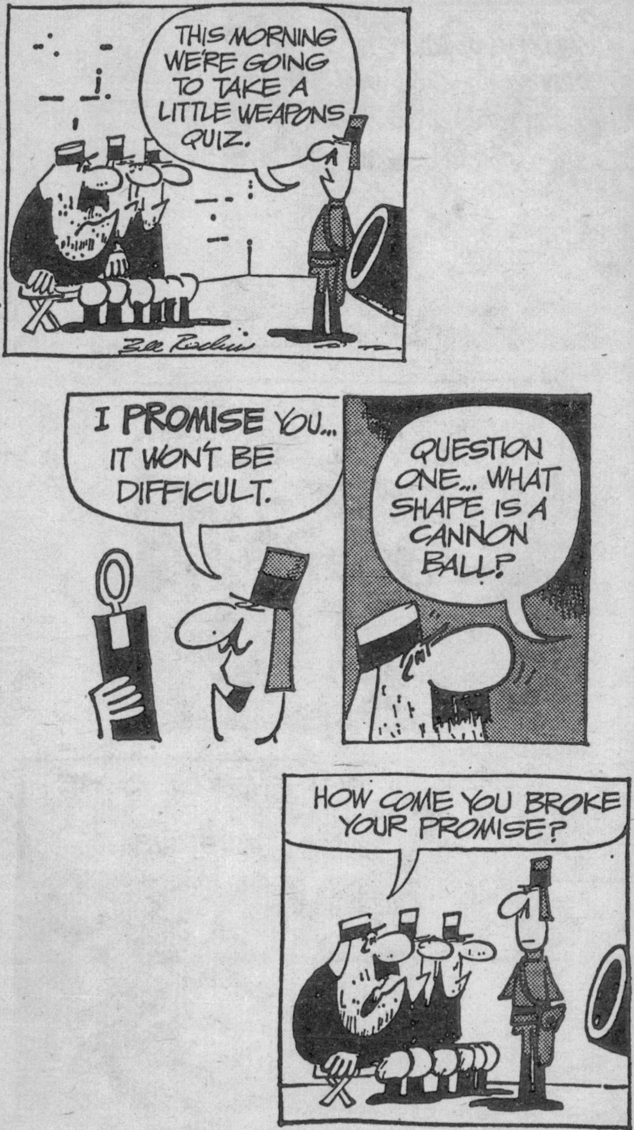
THIS MORNING WE'RE GOING TO TAKE A LITTLE WEAPONS QUIZ.
Bill Rechin
I PROMISE YOU... IT WON'T BE DIFFICULT.
QUESTION ONE... WHAT SHAPE IS A CANNON BALL?
HOW COME YOU BROKE YOUR PROMISE?

wednesday

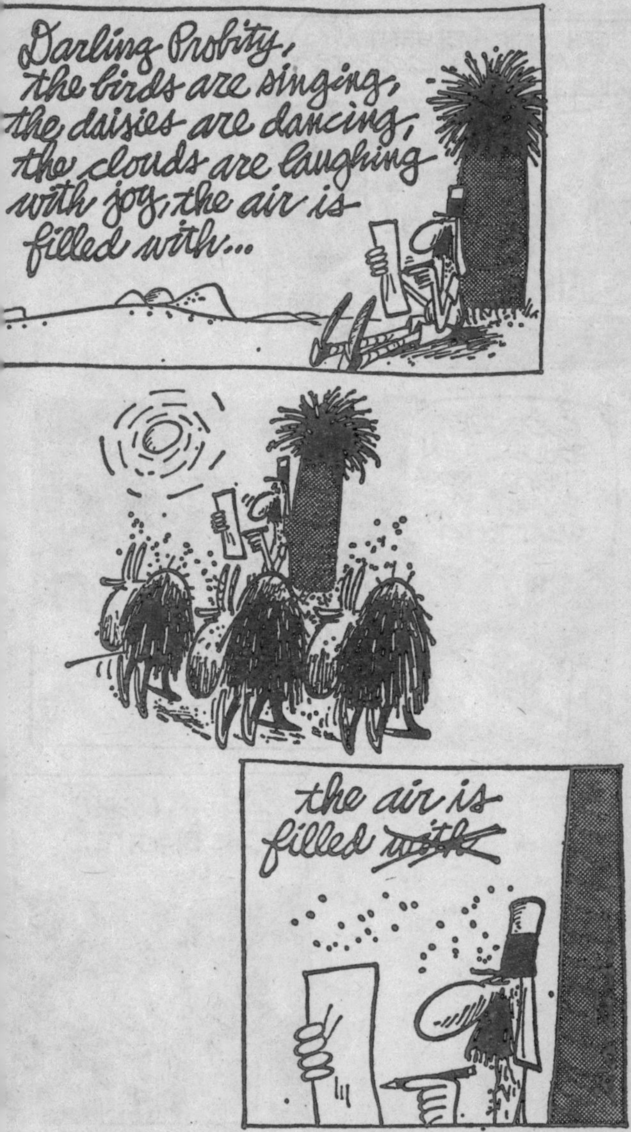
Darling Probity, the birds are singing, the daisies are dancing, the clouds are laughing with joy, the air is filled with...
the air is filled with

thursday

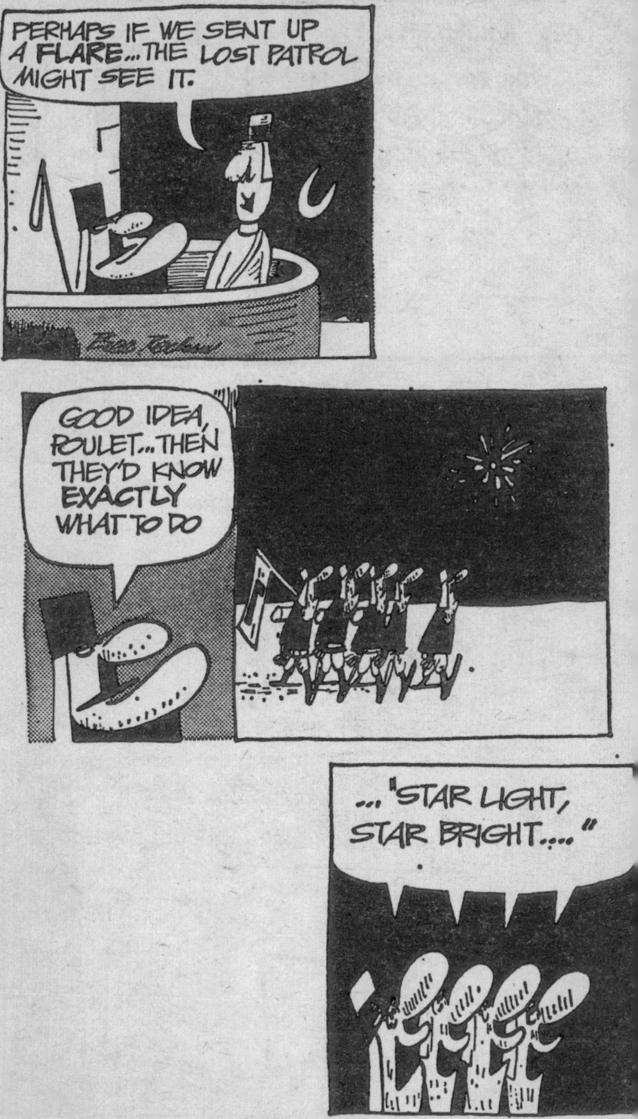
PERHAPS IF WE SENT UP A **FLARE**... THE LOST PATROL MIGHT SEE IT.
GOOD IDEA, POULET... THEN THEY'D KNOW EXACTLY WHAT TO DO
... "STAR LIGHT, STAR BRIGHT...."

friday

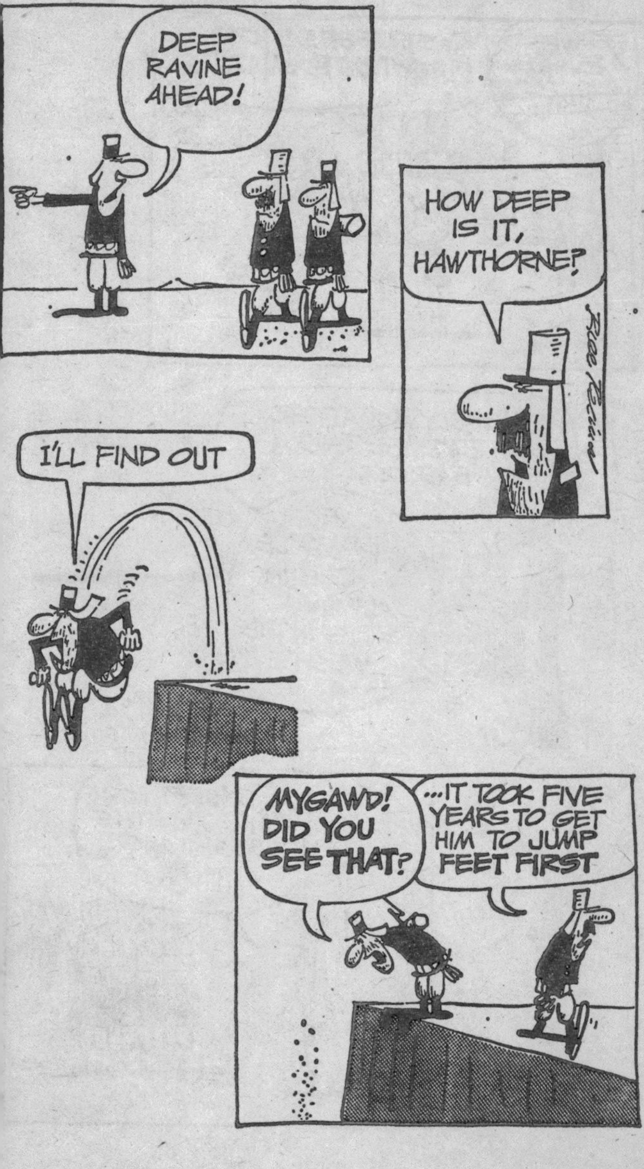

DEEP RAVINE AHEAD!
HOW DEEP IS IT, HAWTHORNE?
I'LL FIND OUT
MYGAWD! DID YOU SEE THAT?
...IT TOOK FIVE YEARS TO GET HIM TO JUMP FEET FIRST

saturday

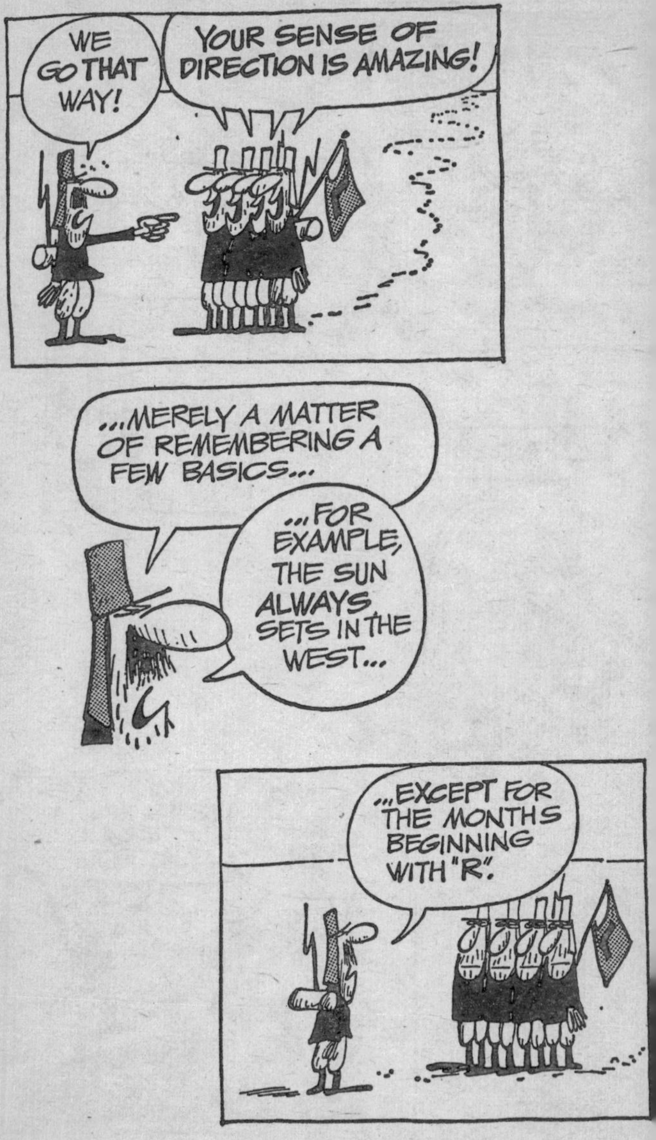
WE GO THAT WAY!
YOUR SENSE OF DIRECTION IS AMAZING!
...MERELY A MATTER OF REMEMBERING A FEW BASICS...
...FOR EXAMPLE, THE SUN ALWAYS SETS IN THE WEST...
...EXCEPT FOR THE MONTHS BEGINNING WITH "R".

monday

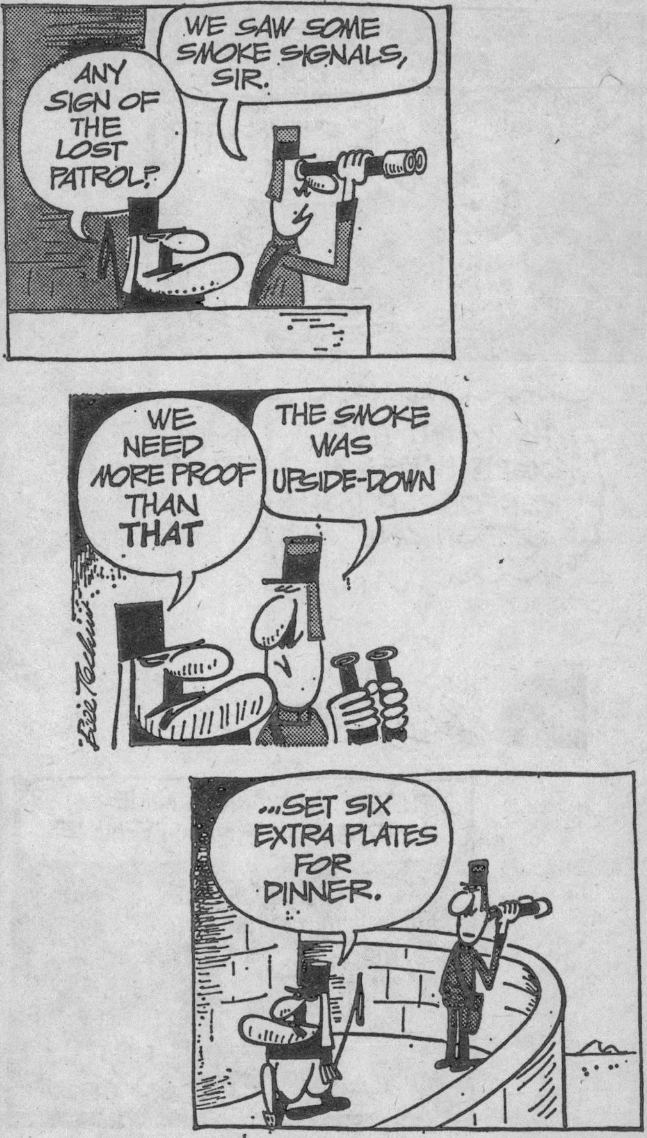
ANY SIGN OF THE LOST PATROL?
WE SAW SOME SMOKE SIGNALS, SIR.
WE NEED MORE PROOF THAN THAT
THE SMOKE WAS UPSIDE-DOWN
...SET SIX EXTRA PLATES FOR DINNER.

tuesday

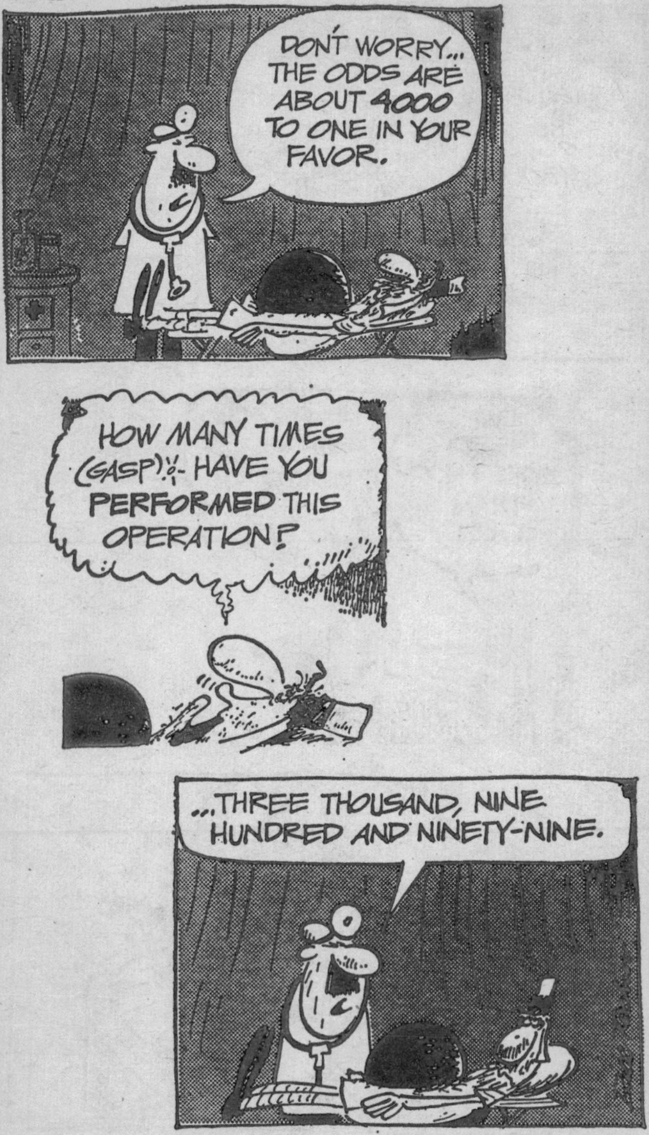
DON'T WORRY... THE ODDS ARE ABOUT 4000 TO ONE IN YOUR FAVOR.
HOW MANY TIMES (GASP) -- HAVE YOU PERFORMED THIS OPERATION?
...THREE THOUSAND, NINE HUNDRED AND NINETY-NINE.

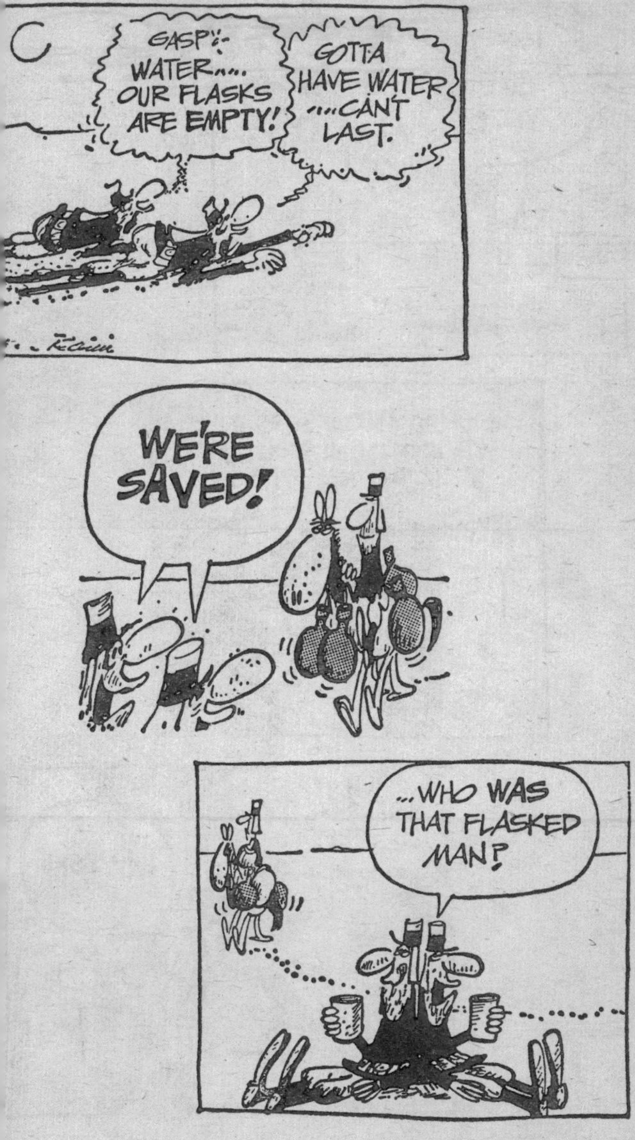
GASP!
WATER..... OUR FLASKS ARE EMPTY!
GOTTA HAVE WATER ....CAN'T LAST.
WE'RE SAVED!
...WHO WAS THAT FLASKED MAN?

thursday

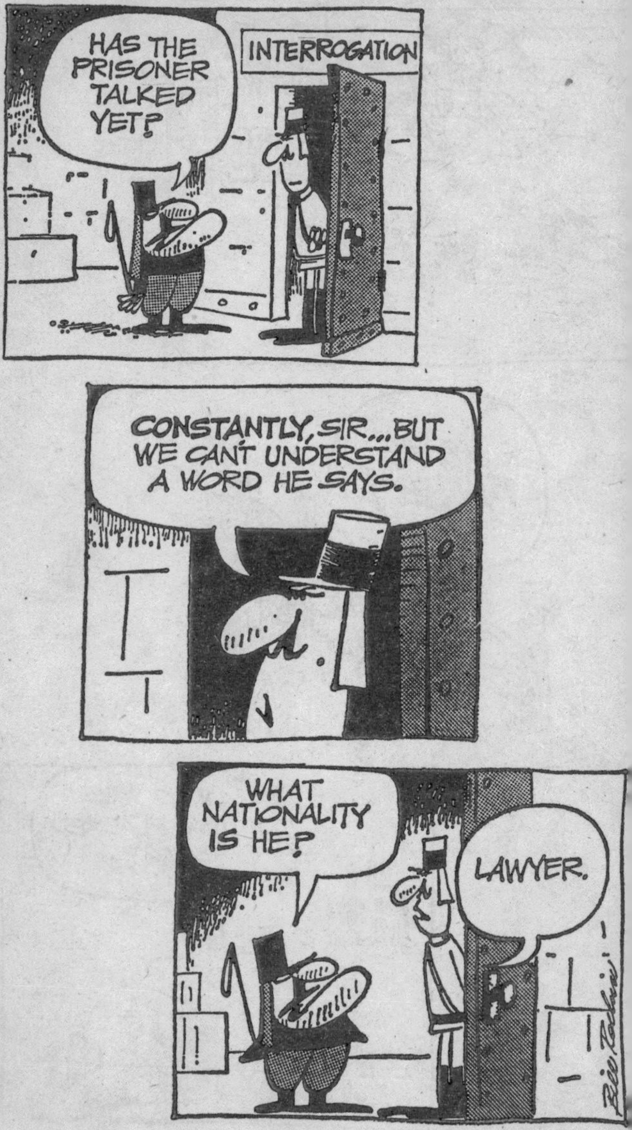
HAS THE PRISONER TALKED YET?
INTERROGATION
CONSTANTLY, SIR... BUT WE CAN'T UNDERSTAND A WORD HE SAYS.
WHAT NATIONALITY IS HE?
LAWYER.

friday

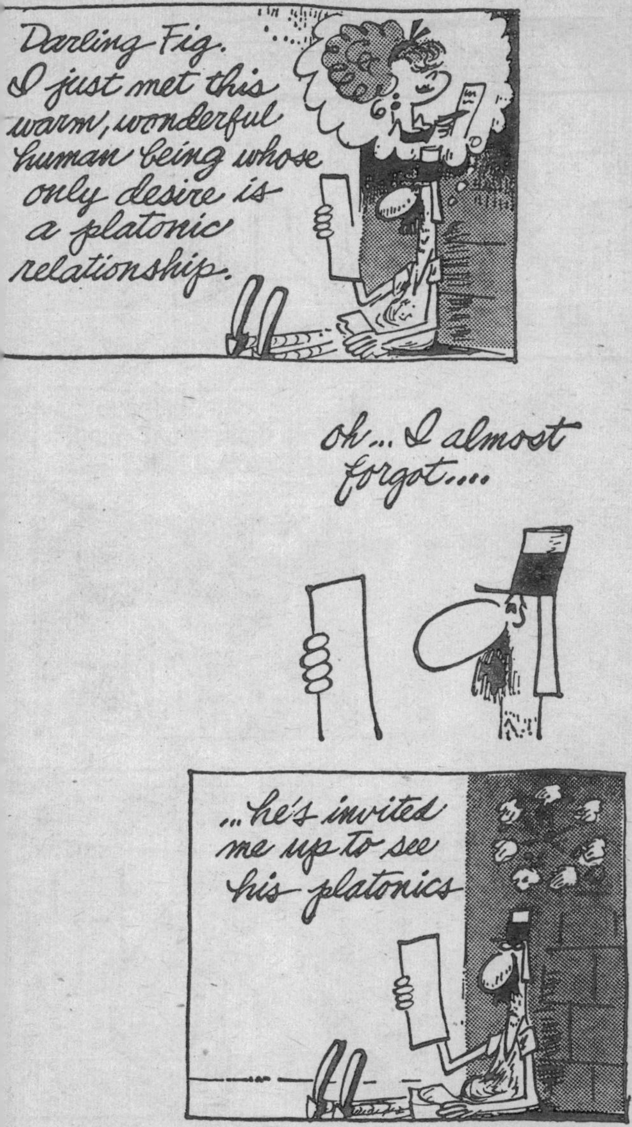
Darling Fig.
I just met this warm, wonderful human being whose only desire is a platonic relationship.
oh... I almost forgot....
...he's invited me up to see his platonics

saturday

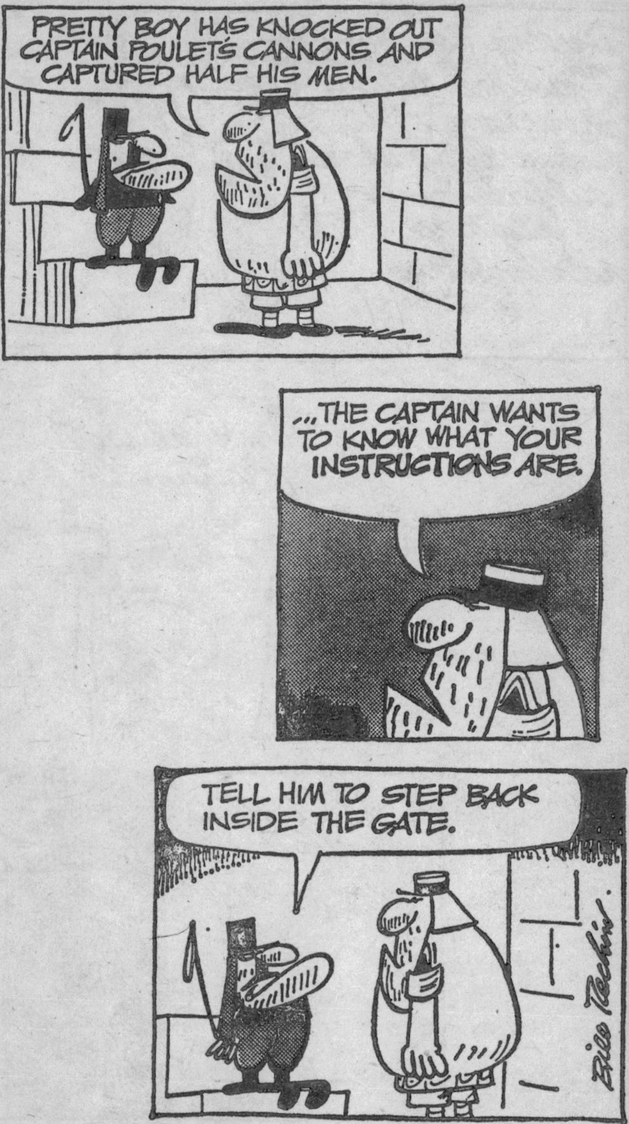
PRETTY BOY HAS KNOCKED OUT CAPTAIN POULET'S CANNONS AND CAPTURED HALF HIS MEN.
...THE CAPTAIN WANTS TO KNOW WHAT YOUR INSTRUCTIONS ARE.
TELL HIM TO STEP BACK INSIDE THE GATE.

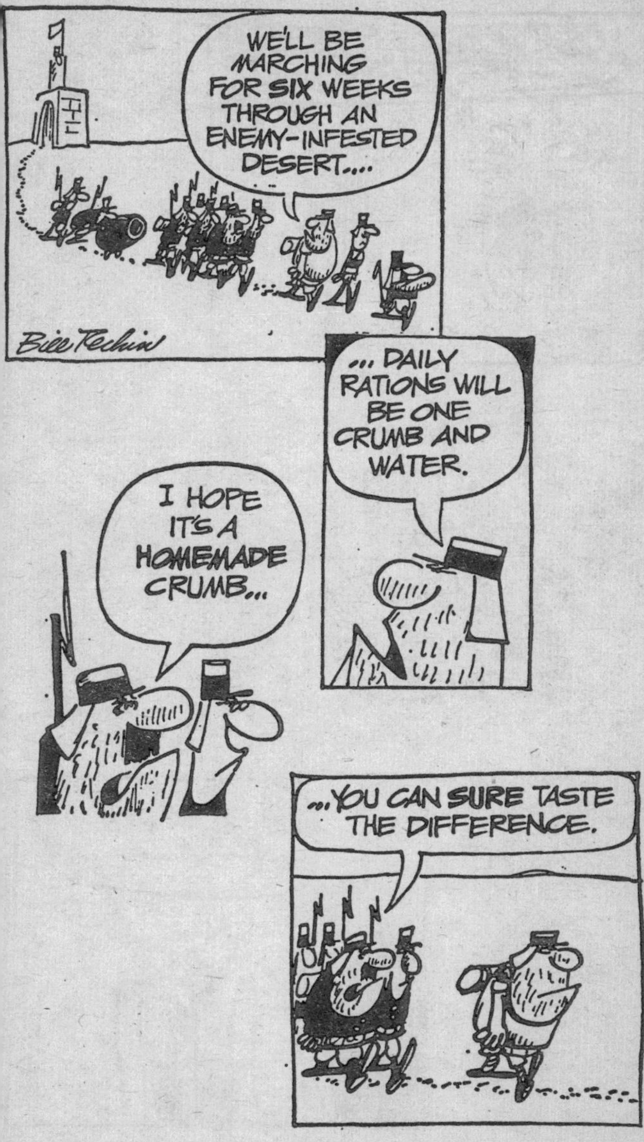
WE'LL BE MARCHING FOR SIX WEEKS THROUGH AN ENEMY-INFESTED DESERT....
Bill Rechin
... DAILY RATIONS WILL BE ONE CRUMB AND WATER.
I HOPE IT'S A HOMEMADE CRUMB...
...YOU CAN SURE TASTE THE DIFFERENCE.

tuesday

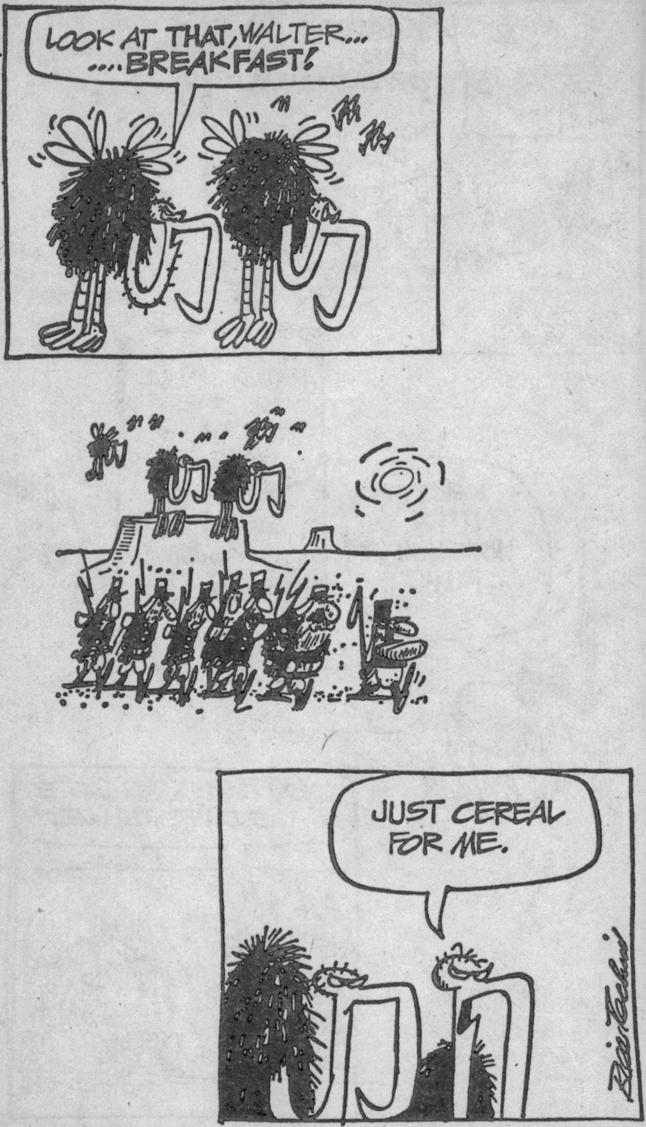
LOOK AT THAT, WALTER...
....BREAKFAST!
JUST CEREAL FOR ME.

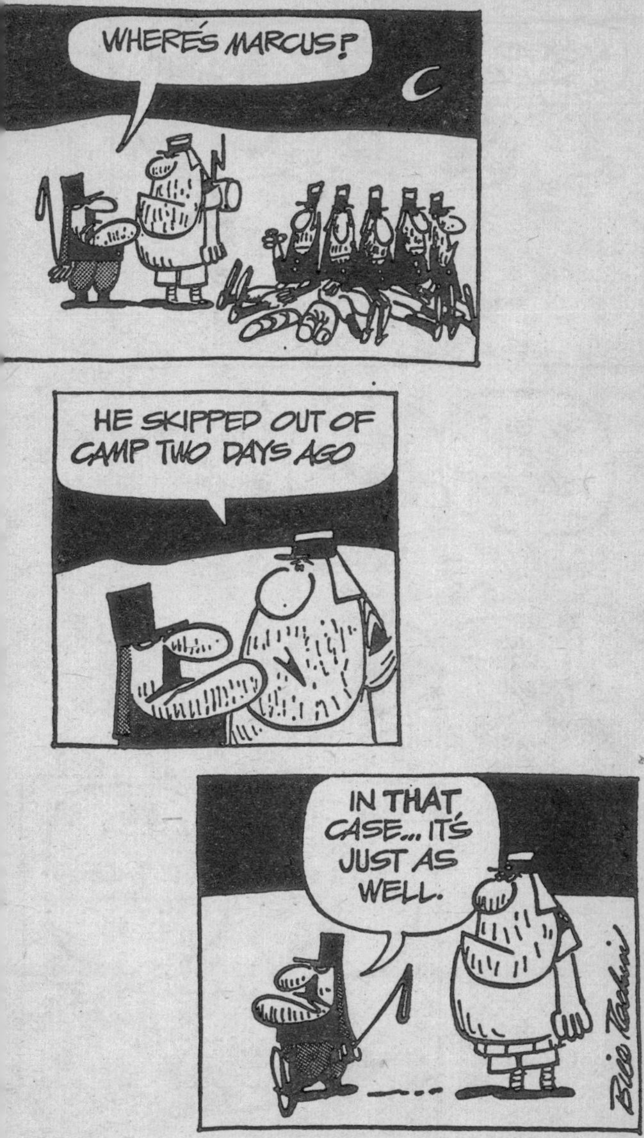
WHERE'S MARCUS?
HE SKIPPED OUT OF CAMP TWO DAYS AGO
IN THAT CASE... IT'S JUST AS WELL.
Bill Rechin

thursday

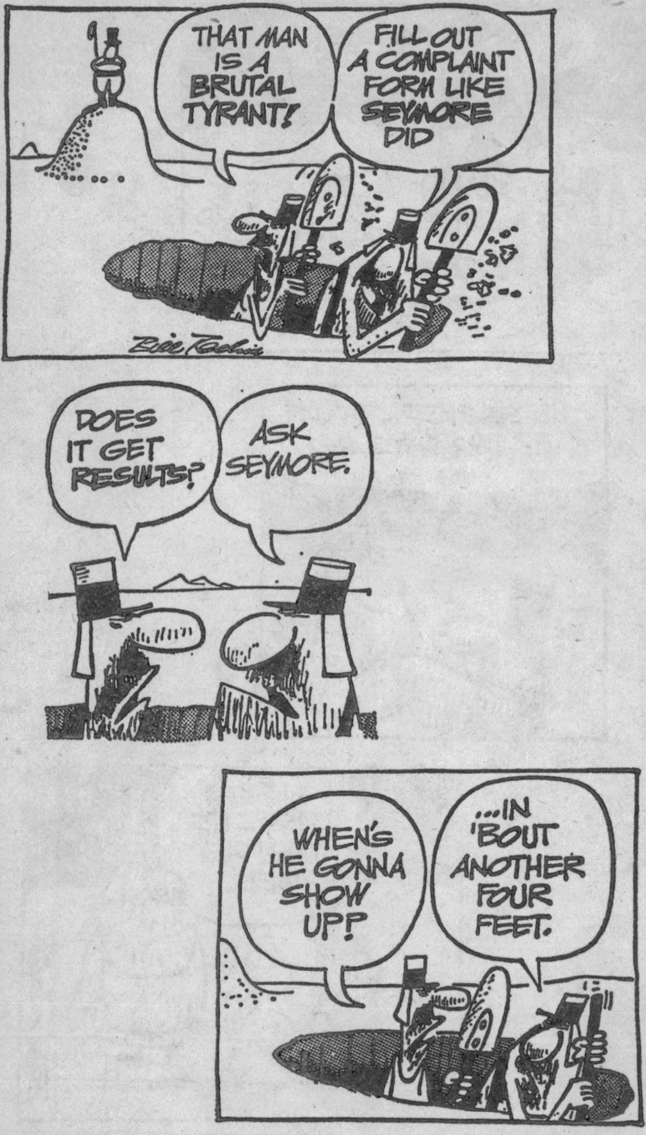
THAT MAN IS A BRUTAL TYRANT!
FILL OUT A COMPLAINT FORM LIKE SEYMORE DID
DOES IT GET RESULTS?
ASK SEYMORE.
WHEN'S HE GONNA SHOW UP?
...IN 'BOUT ANOTHER FOUR FEET.

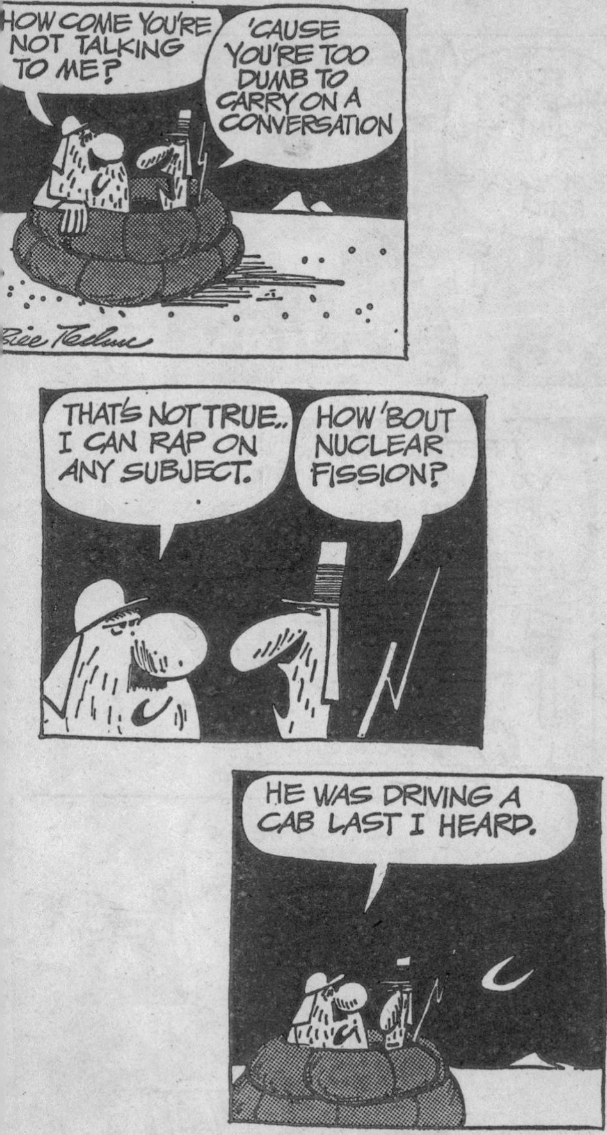
HOW COME YOU'RE NOT TALKING TO ME?
'CAUSE YOU'RE TOO DUMB TO CARRY ON A CONVERSATION
THAT'S NOT TRUE.. I CAN RAP ON ANY SUBJECT.
HOW 'BOUT NUCLEAR FISSION?
HE WAS DRIVING A CAB LAST I HEARD.

saturday

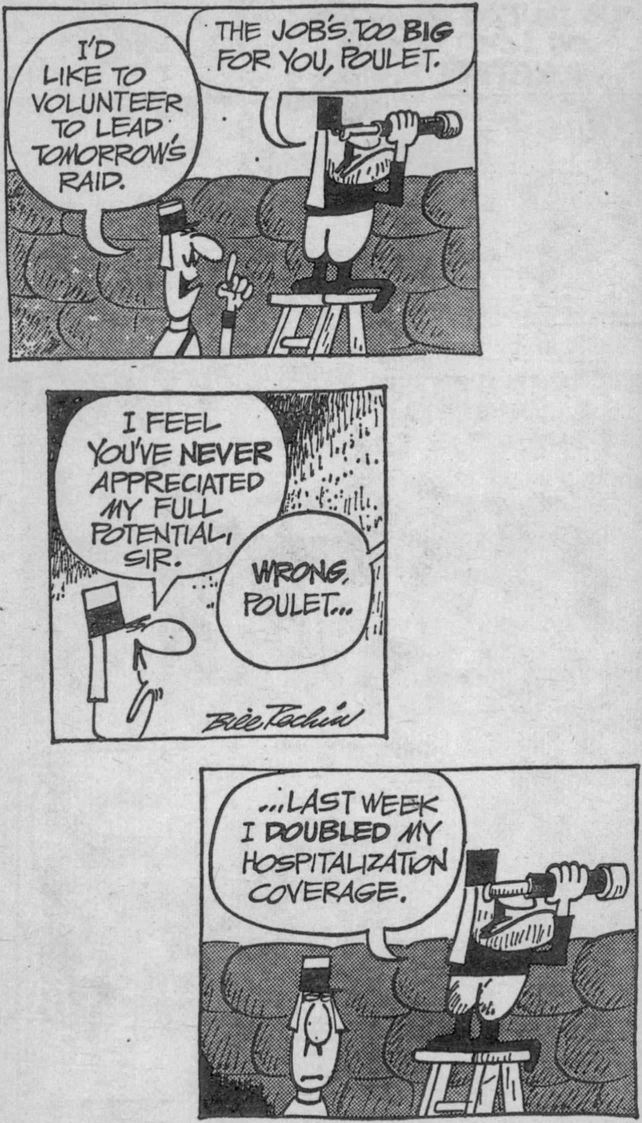
I'D LIKE TO VOLUNTEER TO LEAD TOMORROW'S RAID.
THE JOB'S TOO BIG FOR YOU, POULET.
I FEEL YOU'VE NEVER APPRECIATED MY FULL POTENTIAL, SIR.
WRONG, POULET...
...LAST WEEK I DOUBLED MY HOSPITALIZATION COVERAGE.

monday

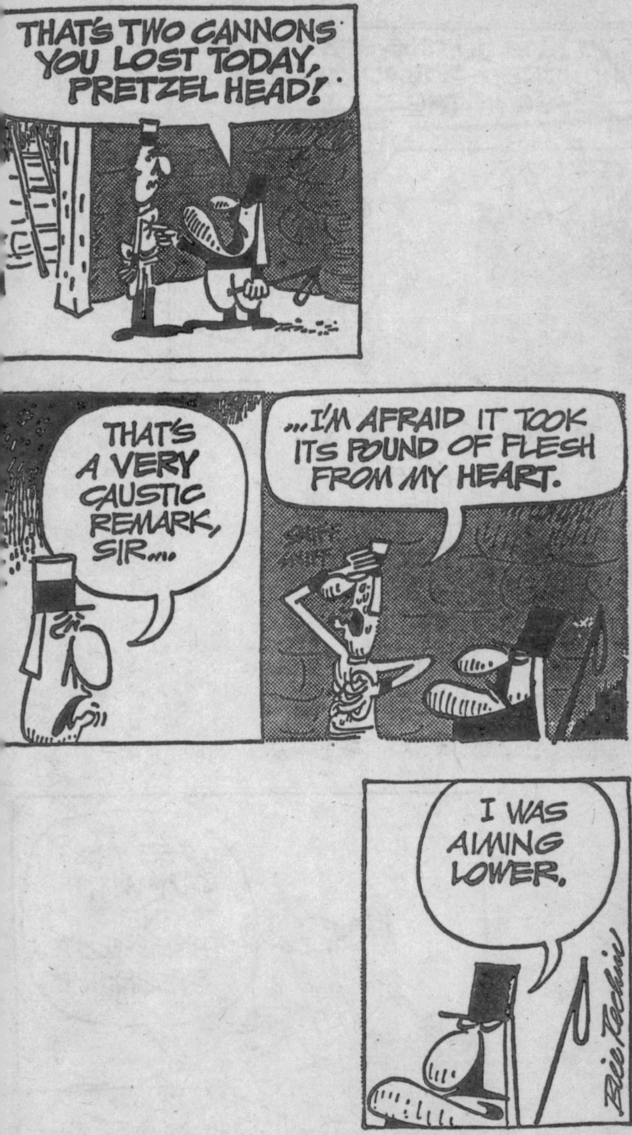
THAT'S TWO CANNONS YOU LOST TODAY, PRETZEL HEAD!
THAT'S A VERY CAUSTIC REMARK, SIR...
...I'M AFRAID IT TOOK ITS POUND OF FLESH FROM MY HEART.
I WAS AIMING LOWER.

tuesday

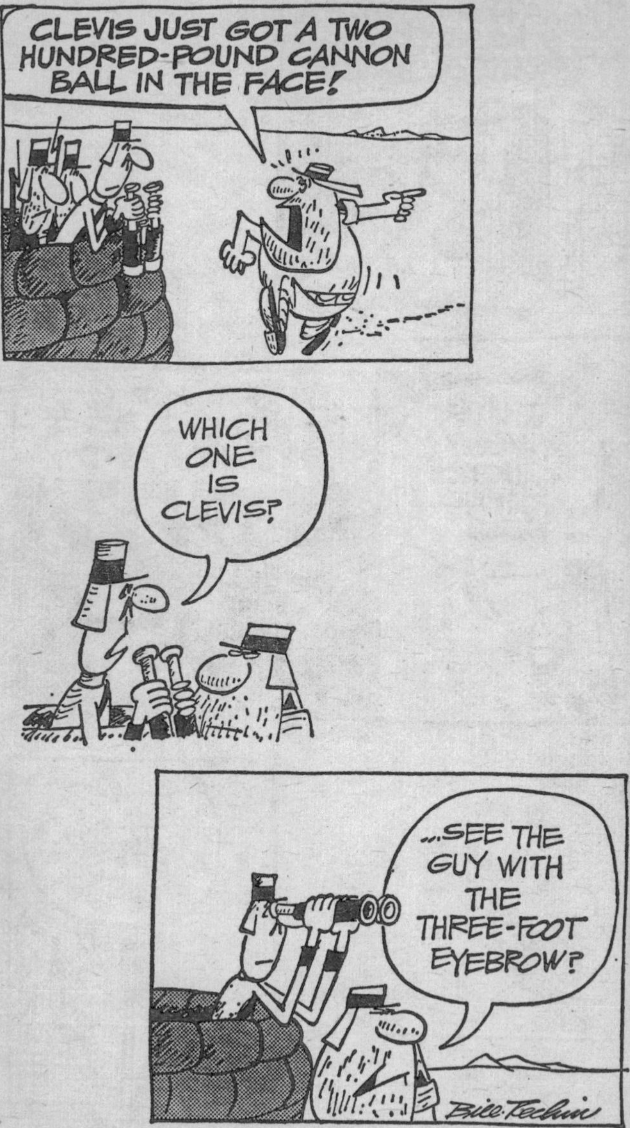

CLEVIS JUST GOT A TWO HUNDRED-POUND CANNON BALL IN THE FACE!
WHICH ONE IS CLEVIS?
...SEE THE GUY WITH THE THREE-FOOT EYEBROW?
Bill Rechin

wednesday

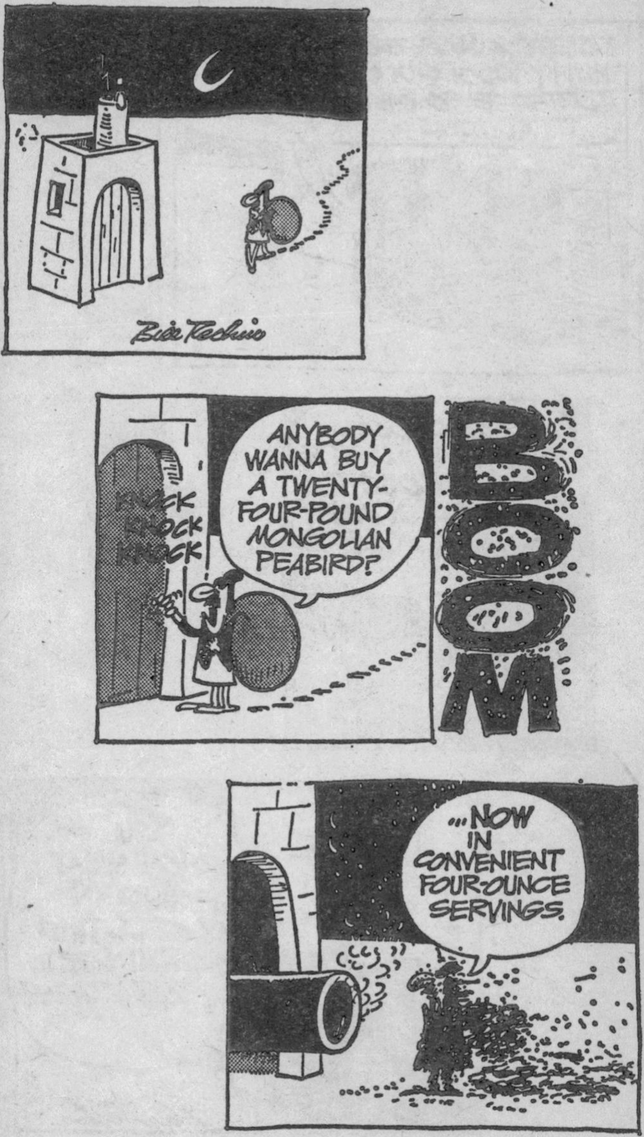
KNOCK KNOCK KNOCK
ANYBODY WANNA BUY A TWENTY-FOUR-POUND MONGOLIAN PEABIRD?
BOOM
...NOW IN CONVENIENT FOUR-OUNCE SERVINGS.

thursday

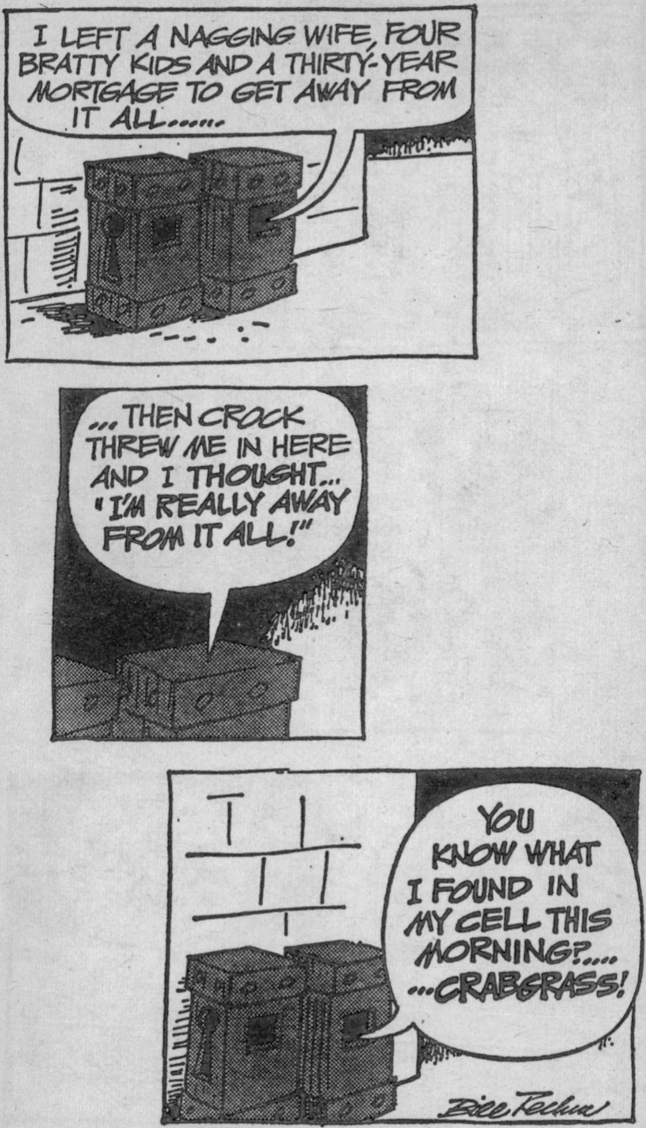
I LEFT A NAGGING WIFE, FOUR BRATTY KIDS AND A THIRTY-YEAR MORTGAGE TO GET AWAY FROM IT ALL......
...THEN CROCK THREW ME IN HERE AND I THOUGHT... "I'M REALLY AWAY FROM IT ALL!"
YOU KNOW WHAT I FOUND IN MY CELL THIS MORNING?.... ...CRABGRASS!
Bill Rechin

friday

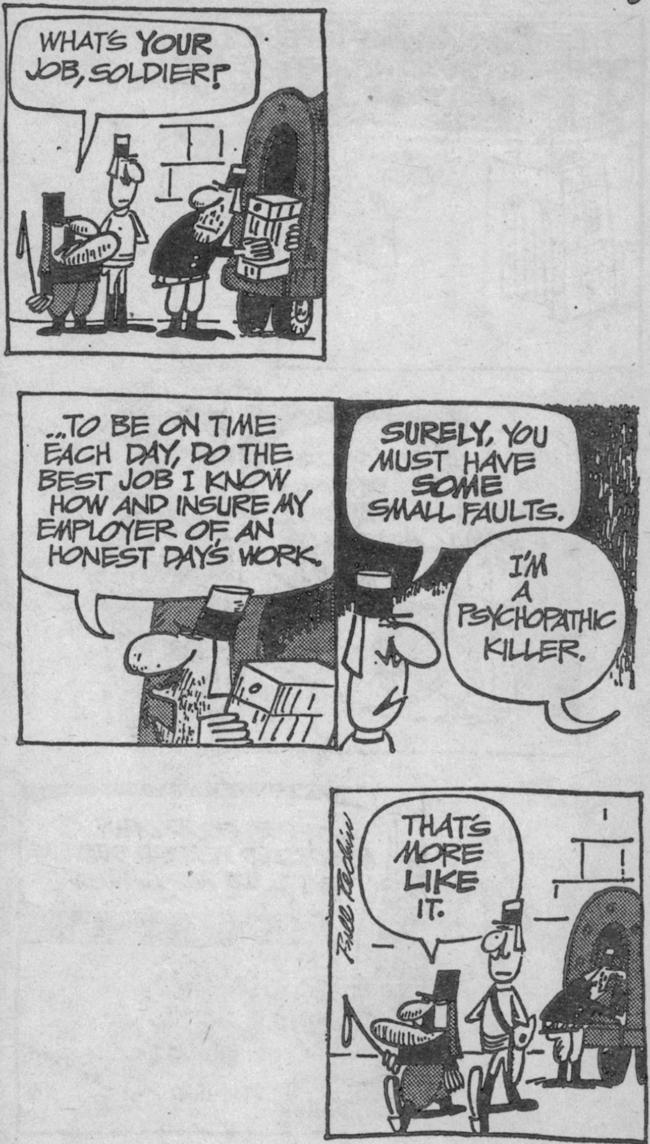
WHAT'S YOUR JOB, SOLDIER?
...TO BE ON TIME EACH DAY, DO THE BEST JOB I KNOW HOW AND INSURE MY EMPLOYER OF AN HONEST DAY'S WORK.
SURELY, YOU MUST HAVE SOME SMALL FAULTS.
I'M A PSYCHOPATHIC KILLER.
THAT'S MORE LIKE IT.

saturday

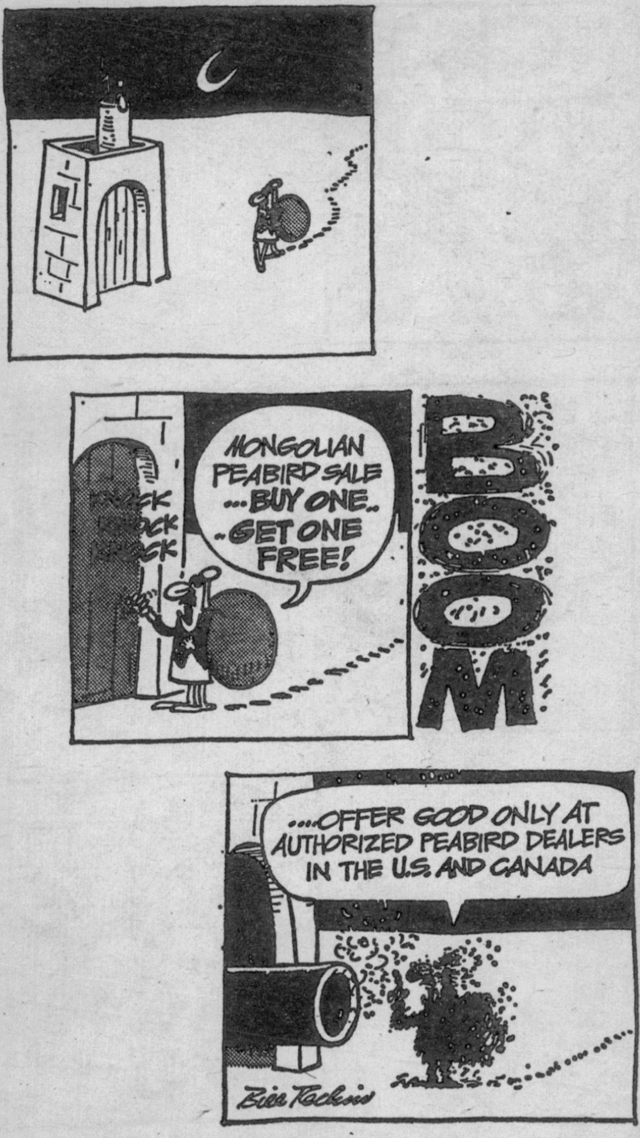
MONGOLIAN PEABIRD SALE ...BUY ONE.. ..GET ONE FREE!
BOOM
....OFFER GOOD ONLY AT AUTHORIZED PEABIRD DEALERS IN THE U.S. AND CANADA
Bill Rechin

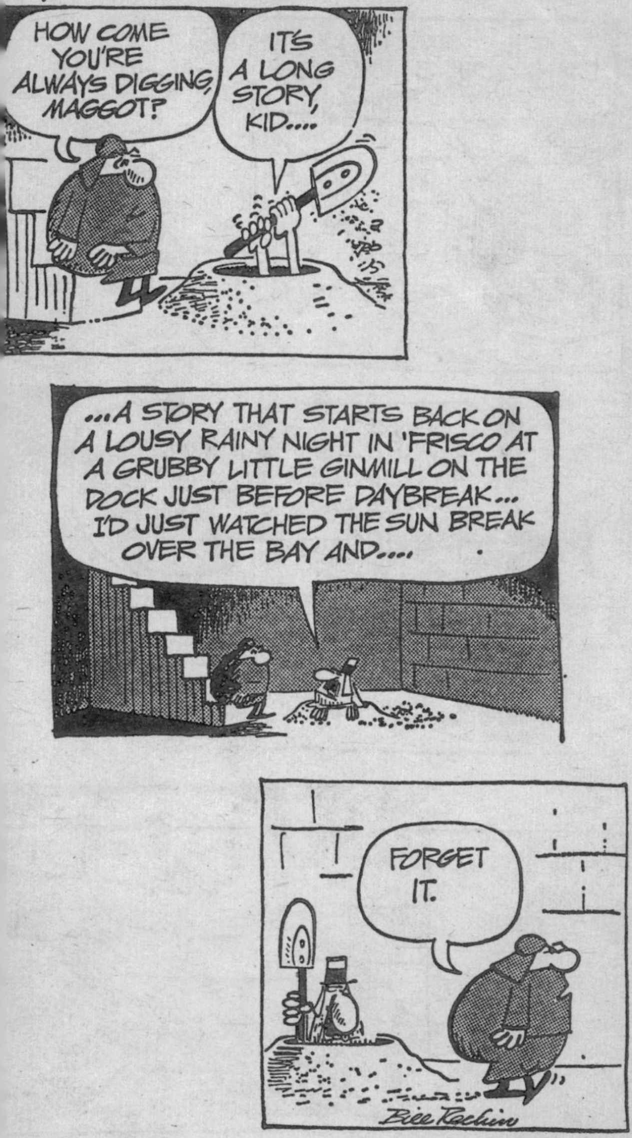
HOW COME YOU'RE ALWAYS DIGGING, MAGGOT?
IT'S A LONG STORY, KID....
...A STORY THAT STARTS BACK ON A LOUSY RAINY NIGHT IN 'FRISCO AT A GRUBBY LITTLE GINMILL ON THE DOCK JUST BEFORE DAYBREAK... I'D JUST WATCHED THE SUN BREAK OVER THE BAY AND....
FORGET IT.
Bill Rechin

tuesday

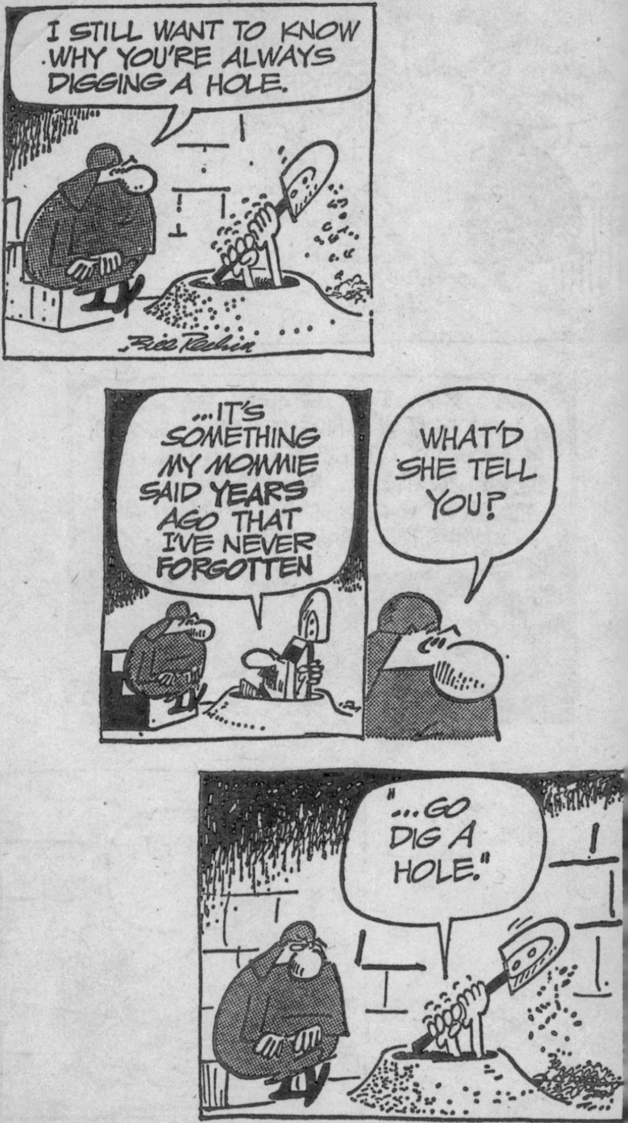
I STILL WANT TO KNOW WHY YOU'RE ALWAYS DIGGING A HOLE.
...IT'S SOMETHING MY MOMMIE SAID YEARS AGO THAT I'VE NEVER FORGOTTEN
WHAT'D SHE TELL YOU?
"...GO DIG A HOLE."

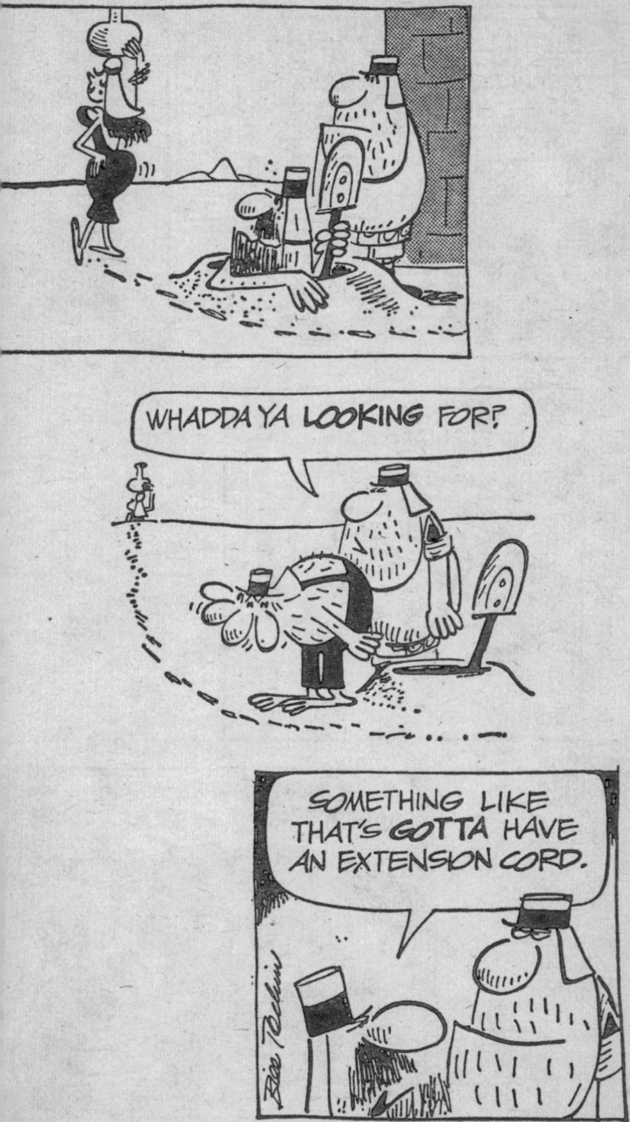
WHADDA YA LOOKING FOR?
SOMETHING LIKE THAT'S GOTTA HAVE AN EXTENSION CORD.
Bil Rechin

thursday

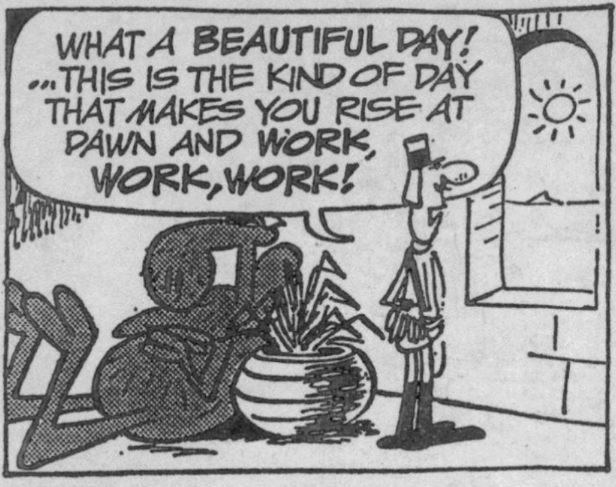
WHAT A BEAUTIFUL DAY! ...THIS IS THE KIND OF DAY THAT MAKES YOU RISE AT DAWN AND WORK, WORK, WORK!

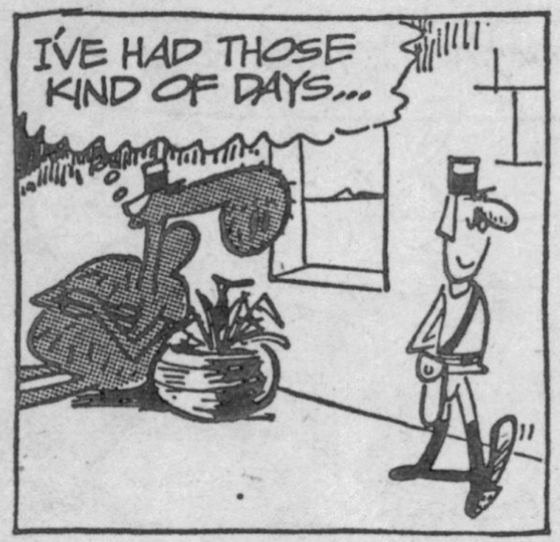
I'VE HAD THOSE KIND OF DAYS...

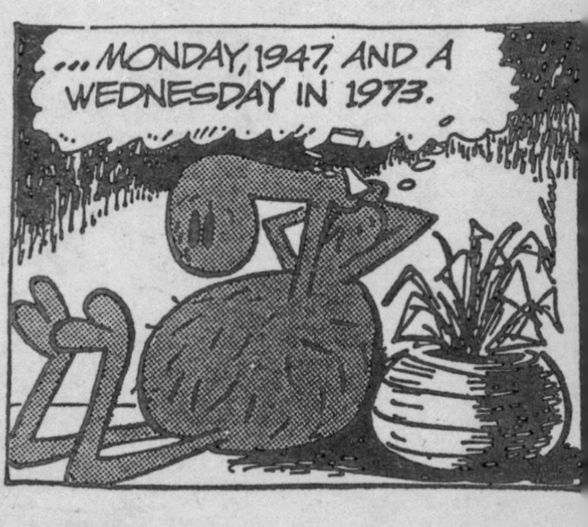
...MONDAY, 1947, AND A WEDNESDAY IN 1973.

friday

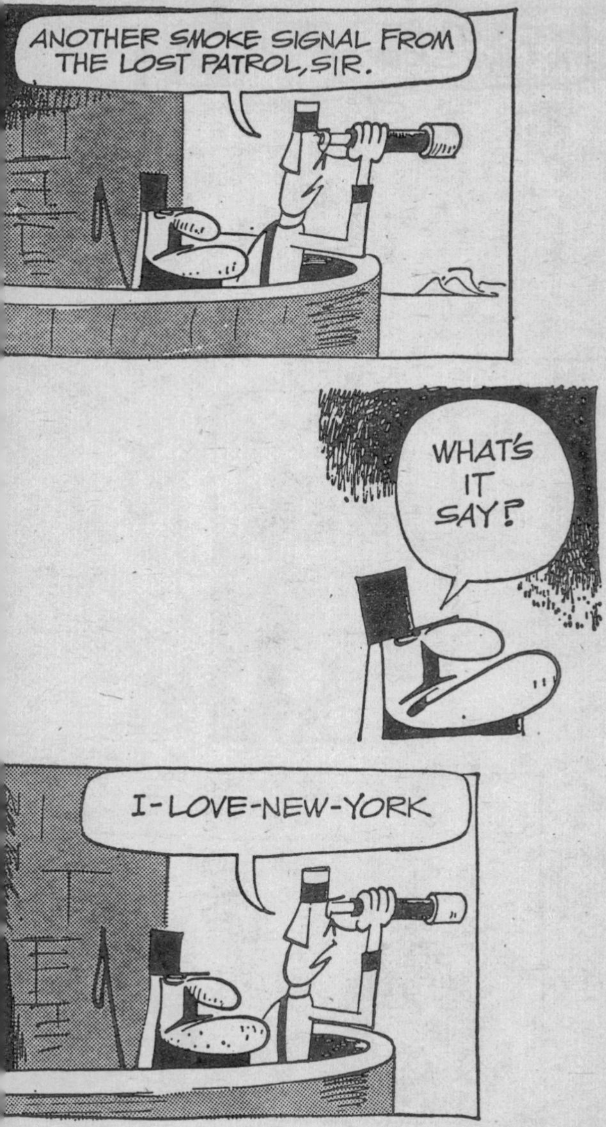
ANOTHER SMOKE SIGNAL FROM THE LOST PATROL, SIR.
WHAT'S IT SAY?
I-LOVE-NEW-YORK

saturday

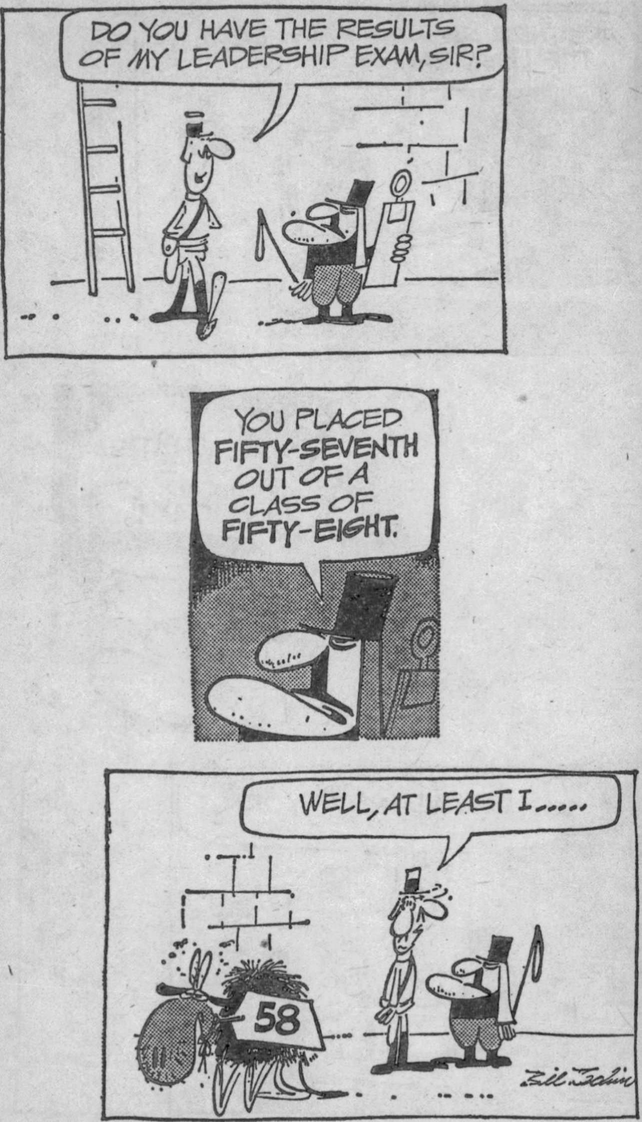
DO YOU HAVE THE RESULTS OF MY LEADERSHIP EXAM, SIR?
YOU PLACED FIFTY-SEVENTH OUT OF A CLASS OF FIFTY-EIGHT.
WELL, AT LEAST I.....
58

monday

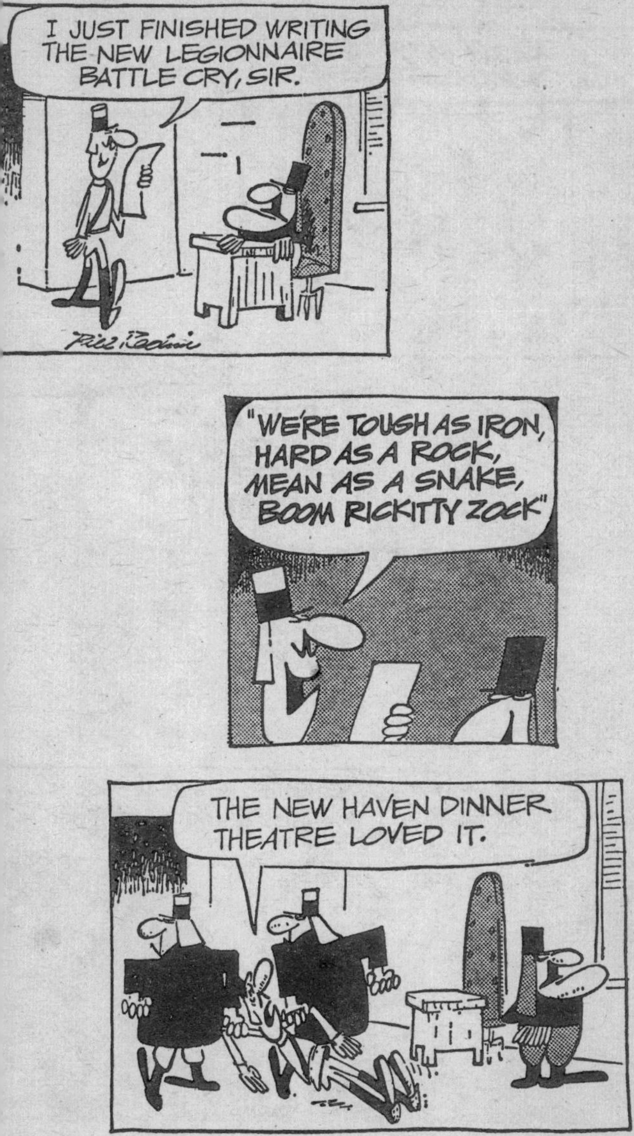
I JUST FINISHED WRITING THE NEW LEGIONNAIRE BATTLE CRY, SIR.
"WE'RE TOUGH AS IRON, HARD AS A ROCK, MEAN AS A SNAKE, BOOM RICKITTY ZOCK"
THE NEW HAVEN DINNER THEATRE LOVED IT.

tuesday

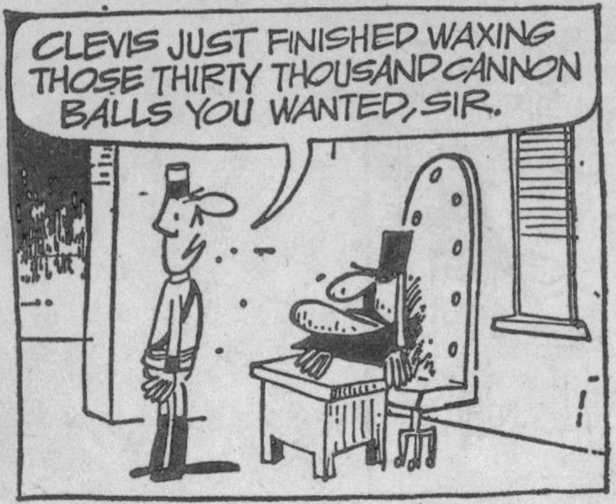
CLEVIS JUST FINISHED WAXING THOSE THIRTY THOUSAND CANNON BALLS YOU WANTED, SIR.

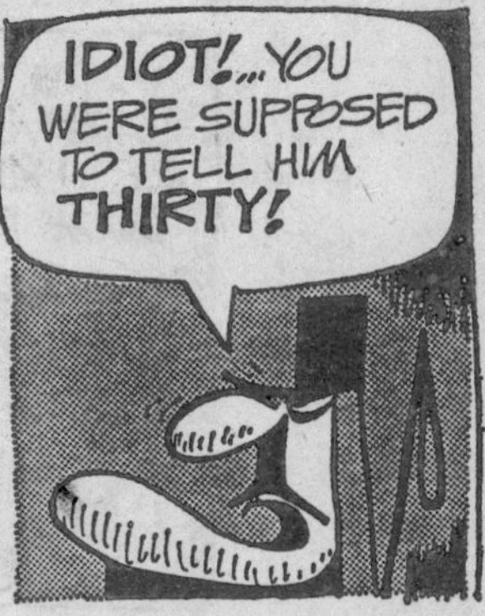
IDIOT!... YOU WERE SUPPOSED TO TELL HIM THIRTY!

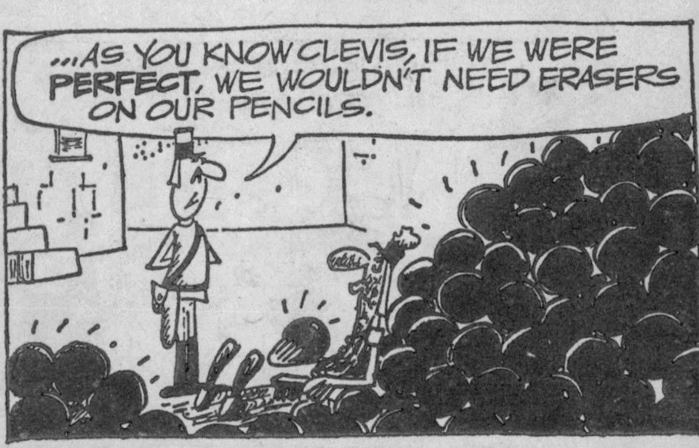
...AS YOU KNOW CLEVIS, IF WE WERE PERFECT, WE WOULDN'T NEED ERASERS ON OUR PENCILS.

wednesday

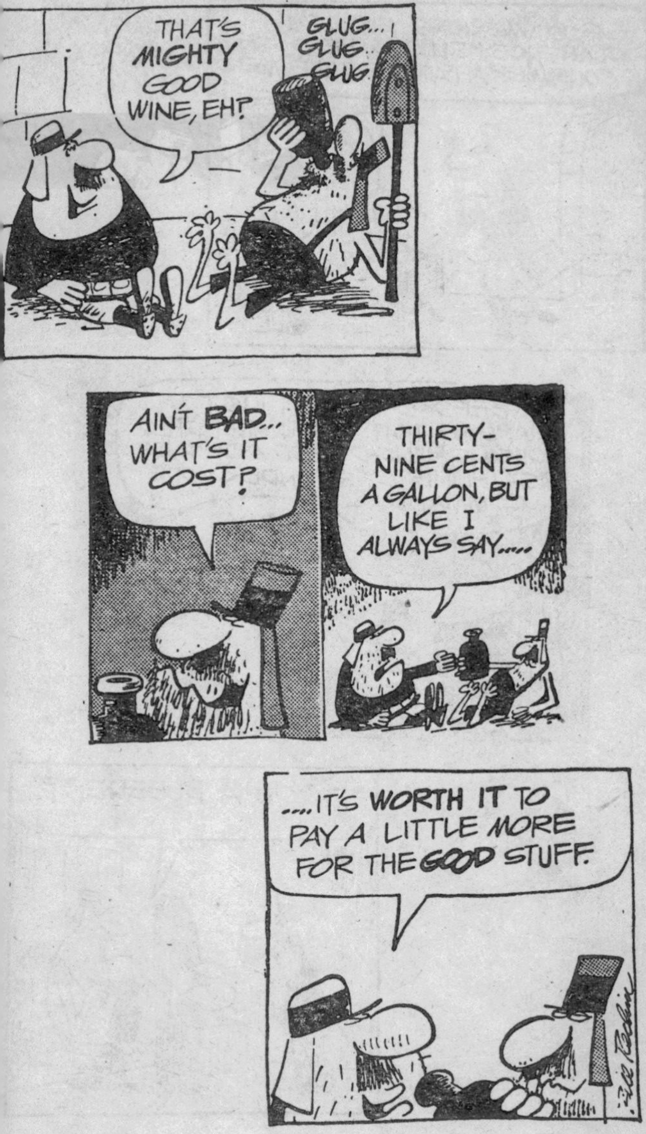
THAT'S MIGHTY GOOD WINE, EH?
GLUG... GLUG... GLUG
AIN'T BAD... WHAT'S IT COST?
THIRTY-NINE CENTS A GALLON, BUT LIKE I ALWAYS SAY.....
....IT'S WORTH IT TO PAY A LITTLE MORE FOR THE GOOD STUFF.

thursday

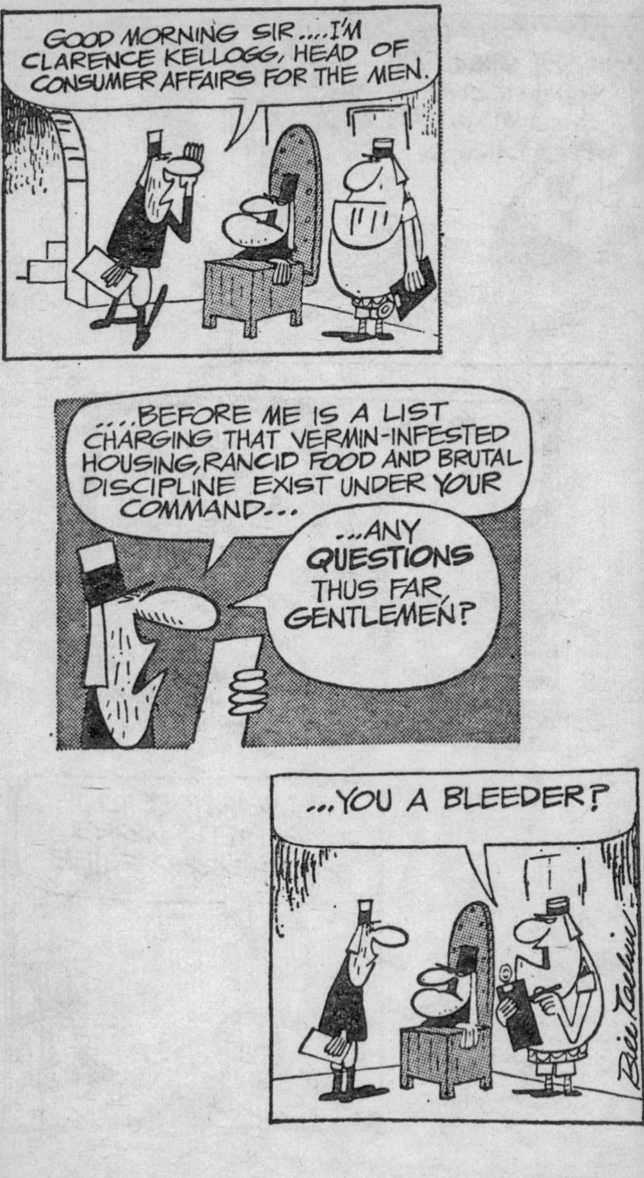
GOOD MORNING SIR....I'M CLARENCE KELLOGG, HEAD OF CONSUMER AFFAIRS FOR THE MEN.
....BEFORE ME IS A LIST CHARGING THAT VERMIN-INFESTED HOUSING, RANCID FOOD AND BRUTAL DISCIPLINE EXIST UNDER YOUR COMMAND...
...ANY QUESTIONS THUS FAR, GENTLEMEN?
...YOU A BLEEDER?
Bill Rechin

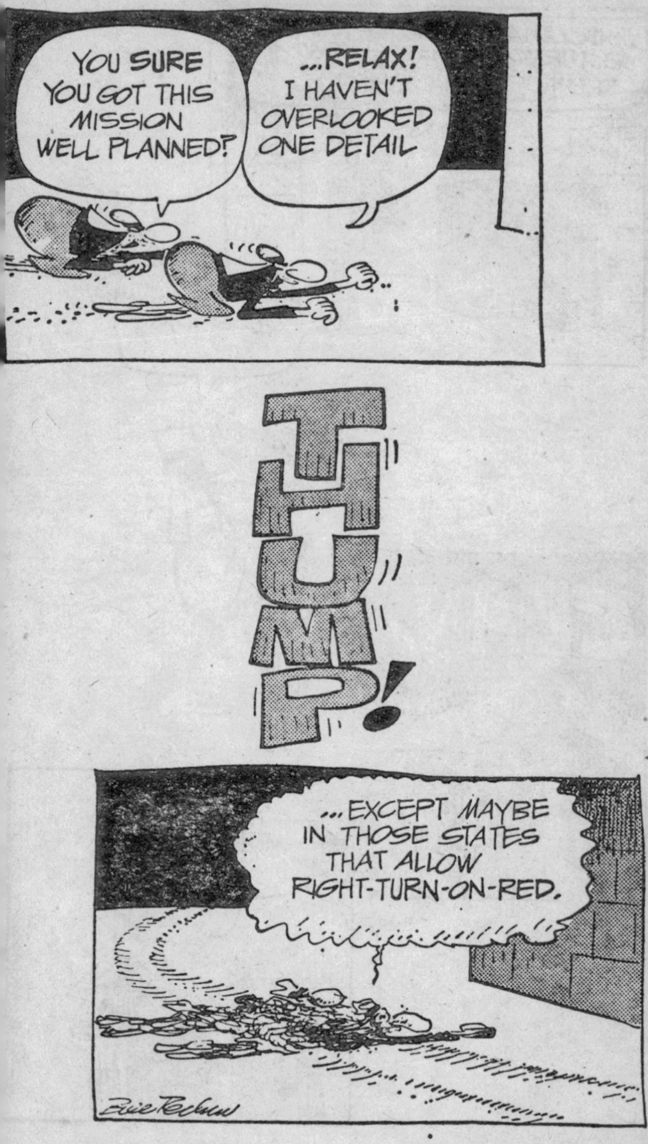
YOU SURE YOU GOT THIS MISSION WELL PLANNED?
...RELAX! I HAVEN'T OVERLOOKED ONE DETAIL
THUMP!
...EXCEPT MAYBE IN THOSE STATES THAT ALLOW RIGHT-TURN-ON-RED.

saturday

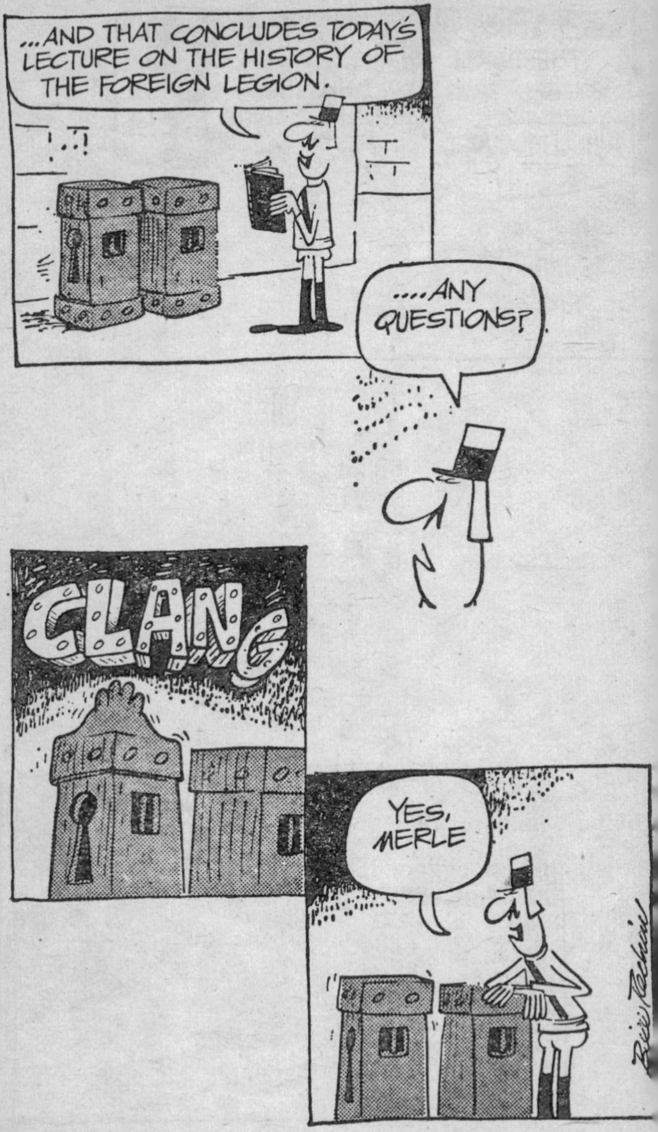
...AND THAT CONCLUDES TODAY'S LECTURE ON THE HISTORY OF THE FOREIGN LEGION.
.....ANY QUESTIONS?
CLANG
YES, MERLE

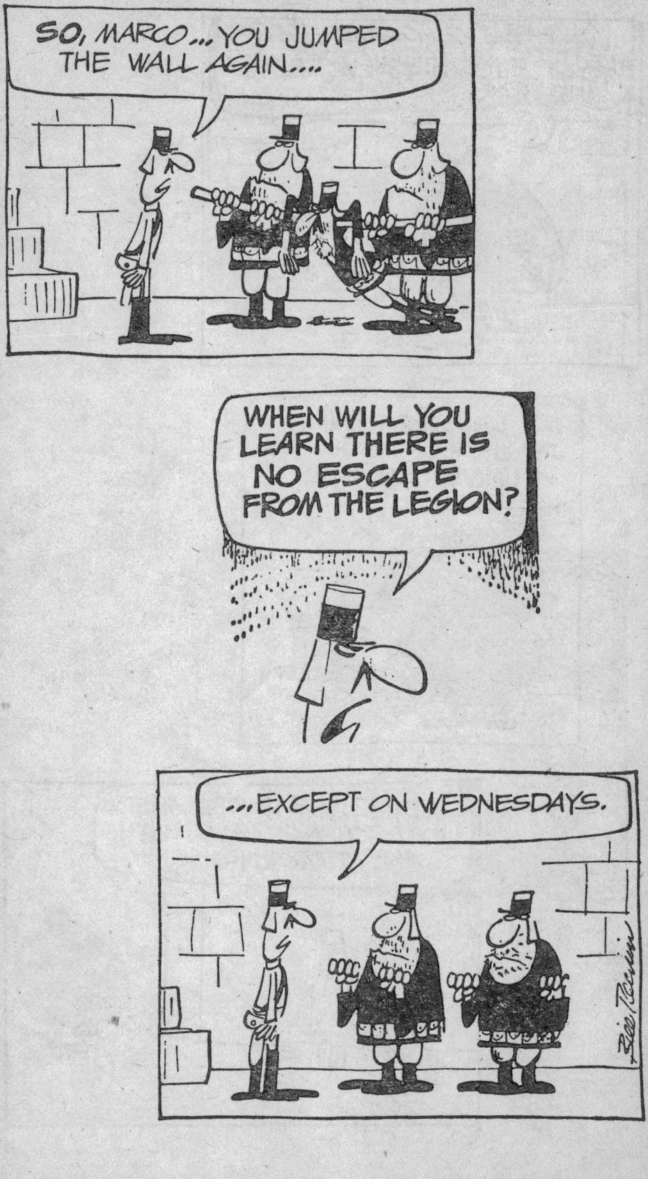
SO, MARCO... YOU JUMPED THE WALL AGAIN....
WHEN WILL YOU LEARN THERE IS NO ESCAPE FROM THE LEGION?
...EXCEPT ON WEDNESDAYS.

tuesday

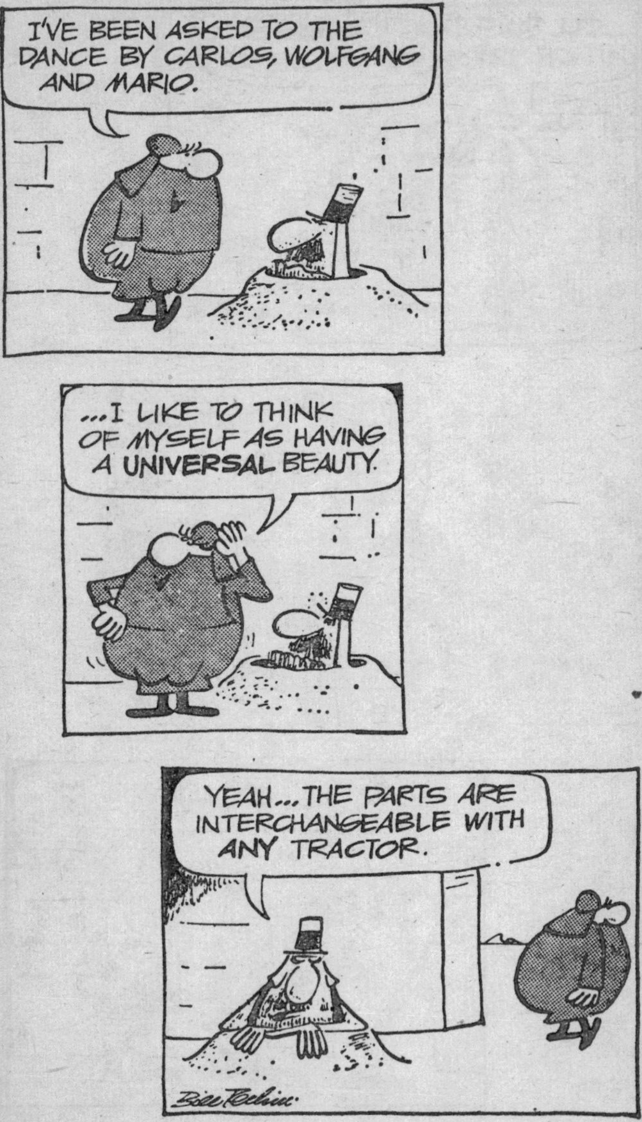
I'VE BEEN ASKED TO THE DANCE BY CARLOS, WOLFGANG AND MARIO.
...I LIKE TO THINK OF MYSELF AS HAVING A UNIVERSAL BEAUTY.
YEAH... THE PARTS ARE INTERCHANGEABLE WITH ANY TRACTOR.
Bill Rechin

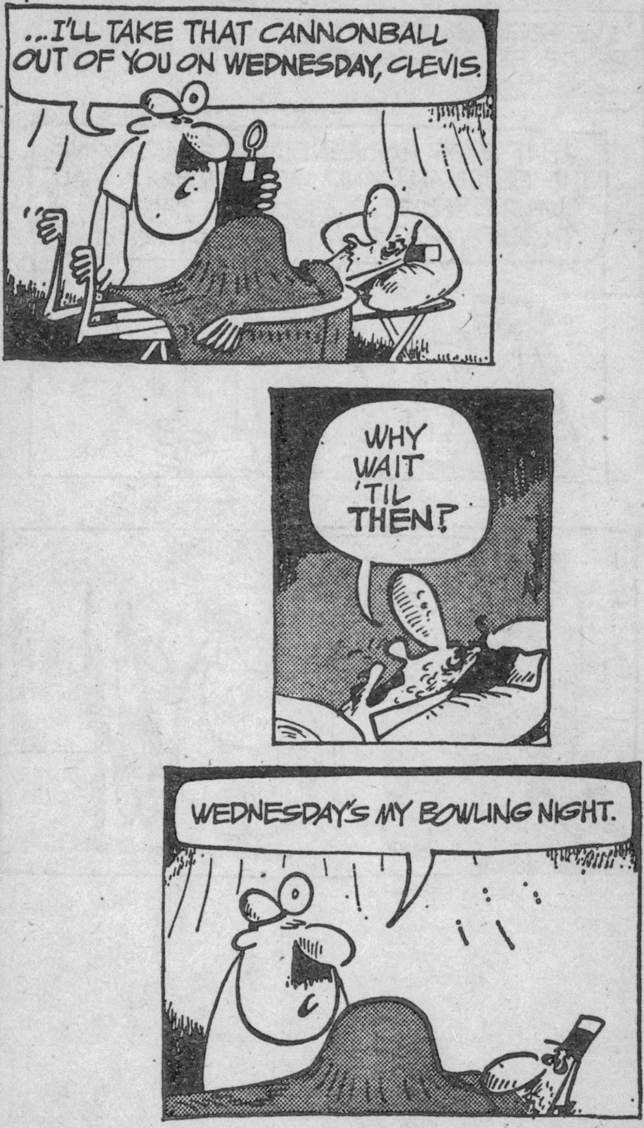
...I'LL TAKE THAT CANNONBALL OUT OF YOU ON WEDNESDAY, CLEVIS.
WHY WAIT 'TIL THEN?
WEDNESDAY'S MY BOWLING NIGHT.

thursday

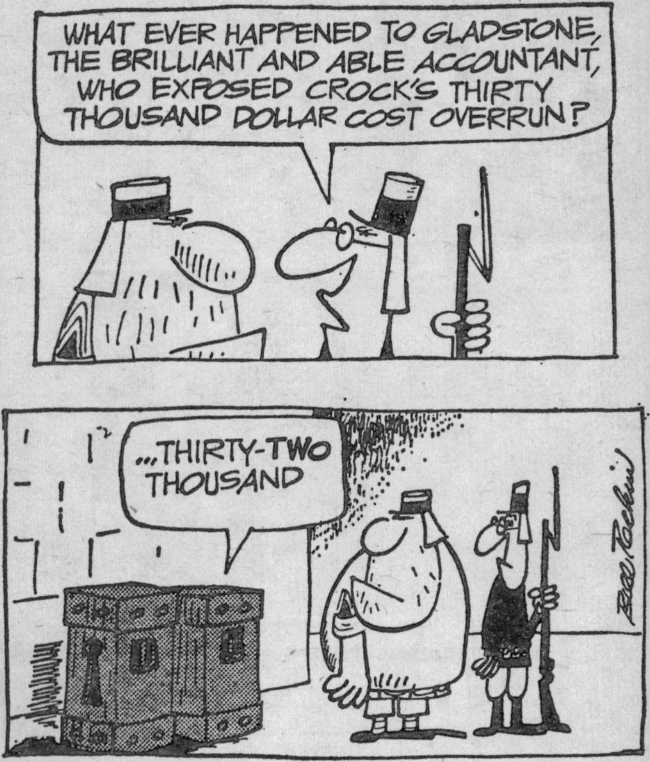
WHAT EVER HAPPENED TO GLADSTONE, THE BRILLIANT AND ABLE ACCOUNTANT, WHO EXPOSED CROCK'S THIRTY THOUSAND DOLLAR COST OVERRUN?
...THIRTY-TWO THOUSAND

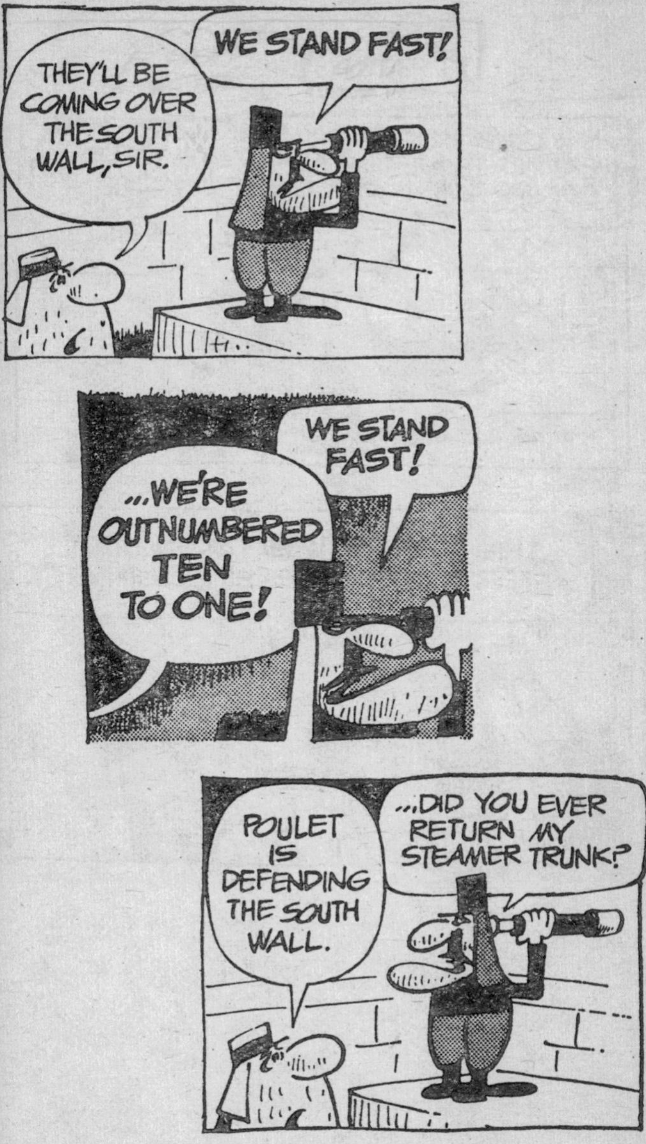
THEY'LL BE COMING OVER THE SOUTH WALL, SIR.
WE STAND FAST!
...WE'RE OUTNUMBERED TEN TO ONE!
WE STAND FAST!
POULET IS DEFENDING THE SOUTH WALL.
...DID YOU EVER RETURN MY STEAMER TRUNK?

saturday

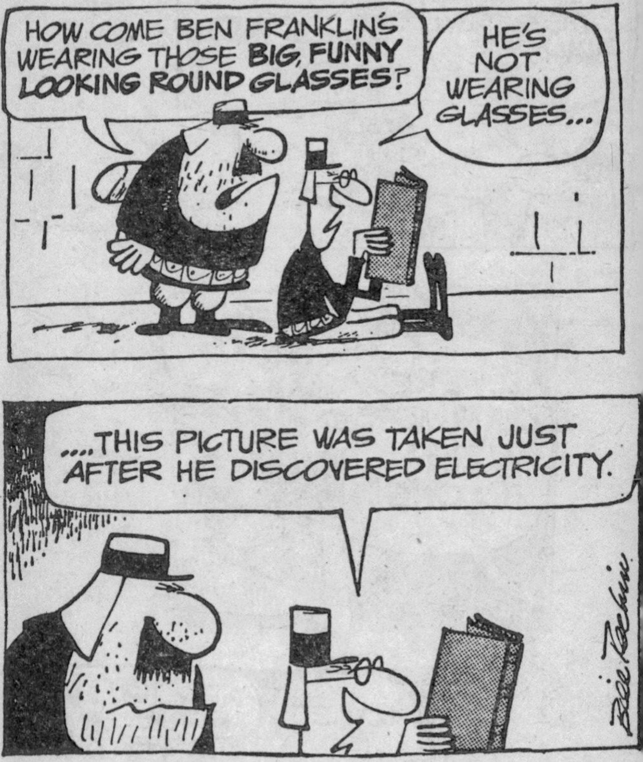
HOW COME BEN FRANKLIN'S WEARING THOSE BIG, FUNNY LOOKING ROUND GLASSES?
HE'S NOT WEARING GLASSES...
....THIS PICTURE WAS TAKEN JUST AFTER HE DISCOVERED ELECTRICITY.
Bil Keane

monday

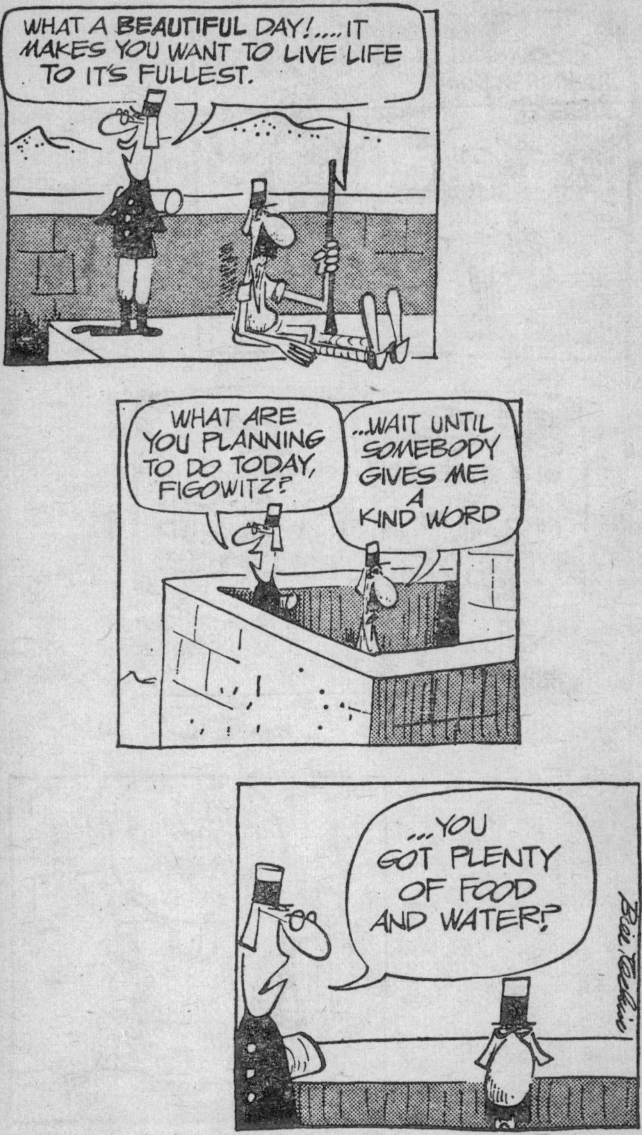
WHAT A BEAUTIFUL DAY!.... IT MAKES YOU WANT TO LIVE LIFE TO IT'S FULLEST.
WHAT ARE YOU PLANNING TO DO TODAY, FIGOWITZ?
...WAIT UNTIL SOMEBODY GIVES ME A KIND WORD
...YOU GOT PLENTY OF FOOD AND WATER?
Bill Rechin

tuesday

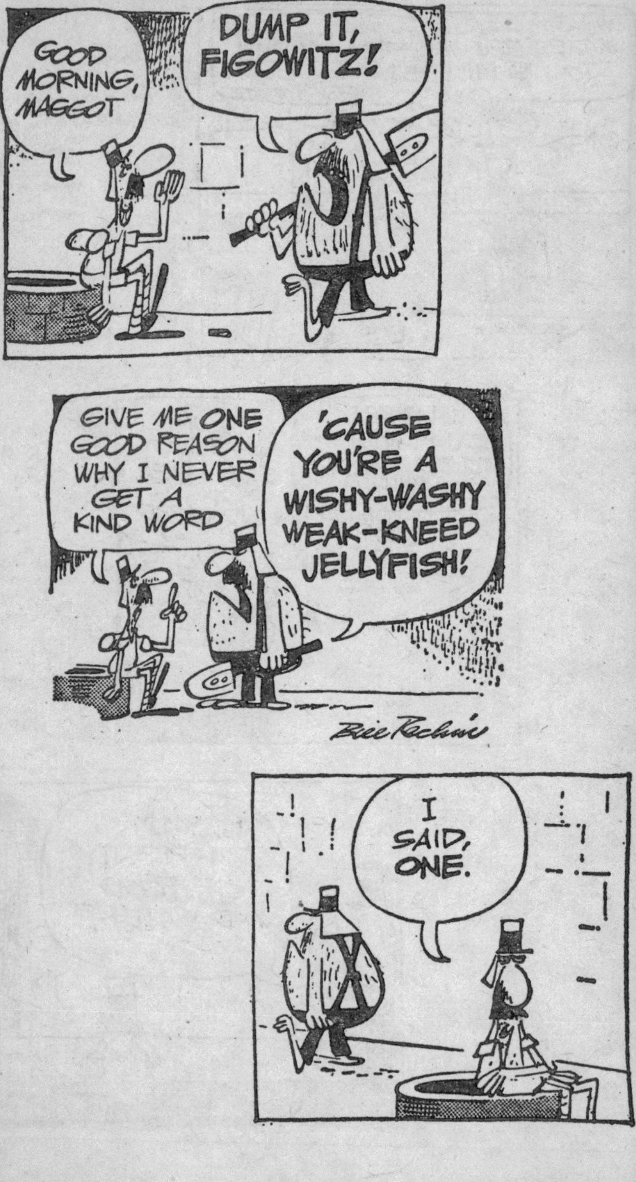
GOOD MORNING, MAGGOT
DUMP IT, FIGOWITZ!
GIVE ME ONE GOOD REASON WHY I NEVER GET A KIND WORD
'CAUSE YOU'RE A WISHY-WASHY WEAK-KNEED JELLYFISH!
I SAID, ONE.

wednesday

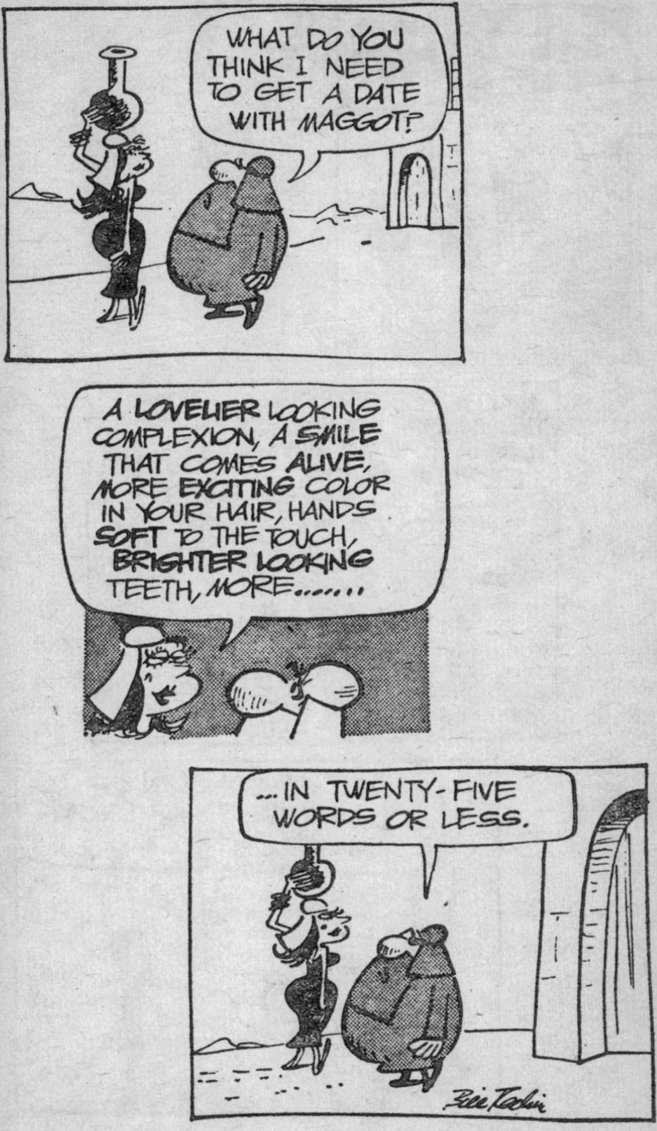
WHAT DO YOU THINK I NEED TO GET A DATE WITH MAGGOT?
A LOVELIER LOOKING COMPLEXION, A SMILE THAT COMES ALIVE, MORE EXCITING COLOR IN YOUR HAIR, HANDS SOFT TO THE TOUCH, BRIGHTER LOOKING TEETH, MORE......
...IN TWENTY-FIVE WORDS OR LESS.

thursday

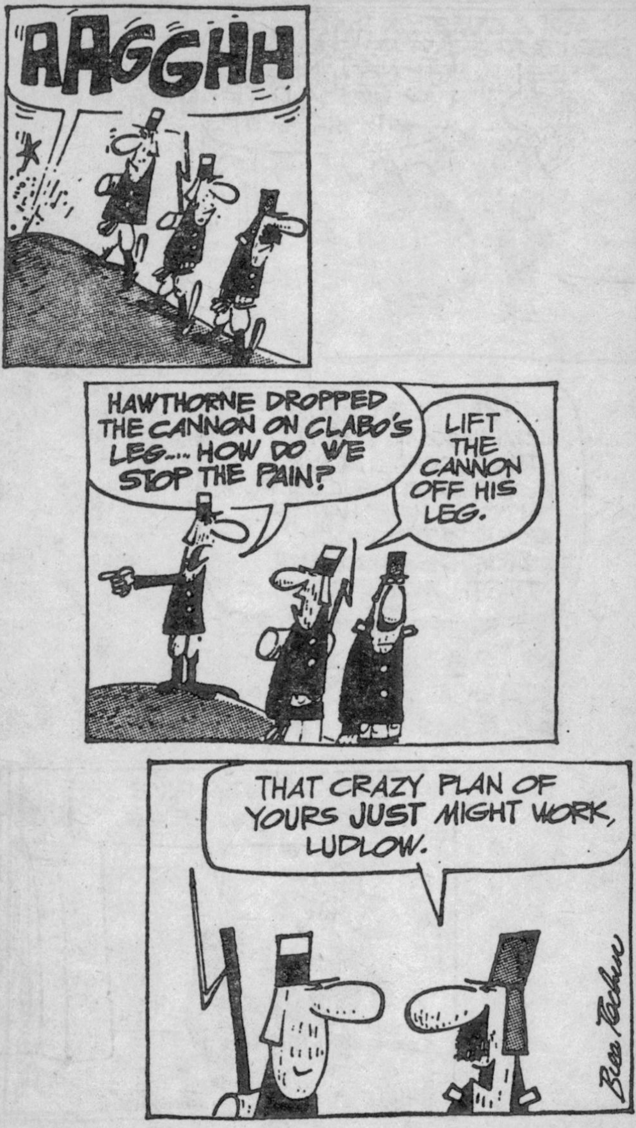

AAGGHH
HAWTHORNE DROPPED THE CANNON ON CLABO'S LEG.... HOW DO WE STOP THE PAIN?
LIFT THE CANNON OFF HIS LEG.
THAT CRAZY PLAN OF YOURS JUST MIGHT WORK, LUDLOW.

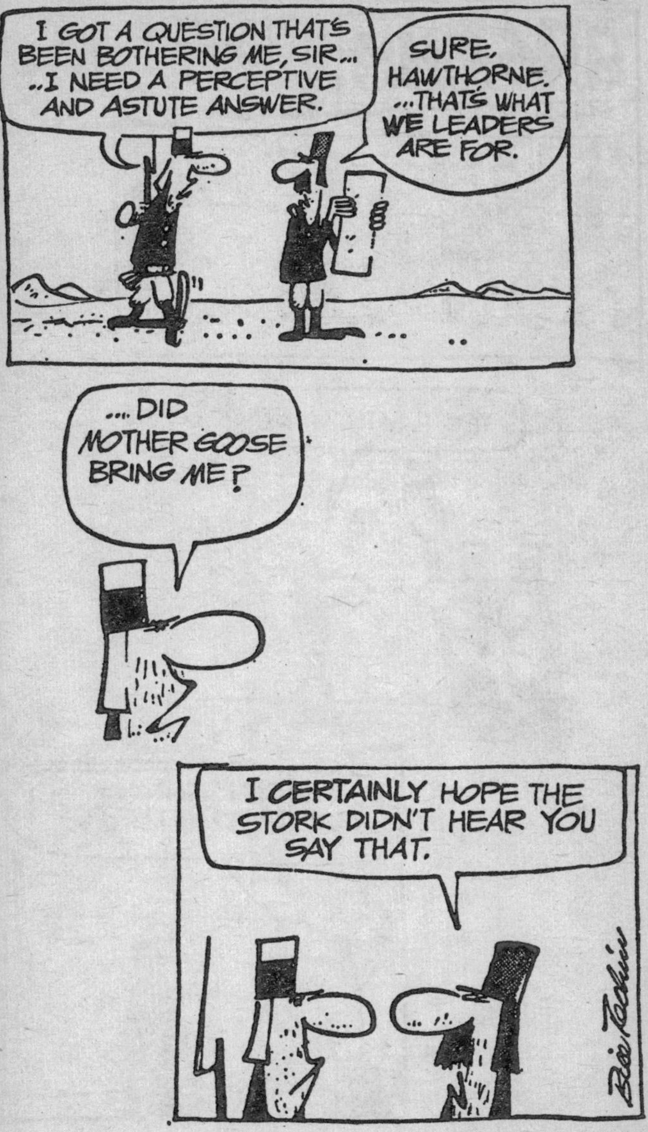
I GOT A QUESTION THAT'S BEEN BOTHERING ME, SIR... ..I NEED A PERCEPTIVE AND ASTUTE ANSWER.
SURE, HAWTHORNE. ...THAT'S WHAT WE LEADERS ARE FOR.
....DID MOTHER GOOSE BRING ME?
I CERTAINLY HOPE THE STORK DIDN'T HEAR YOU SAY THAT.

saturday

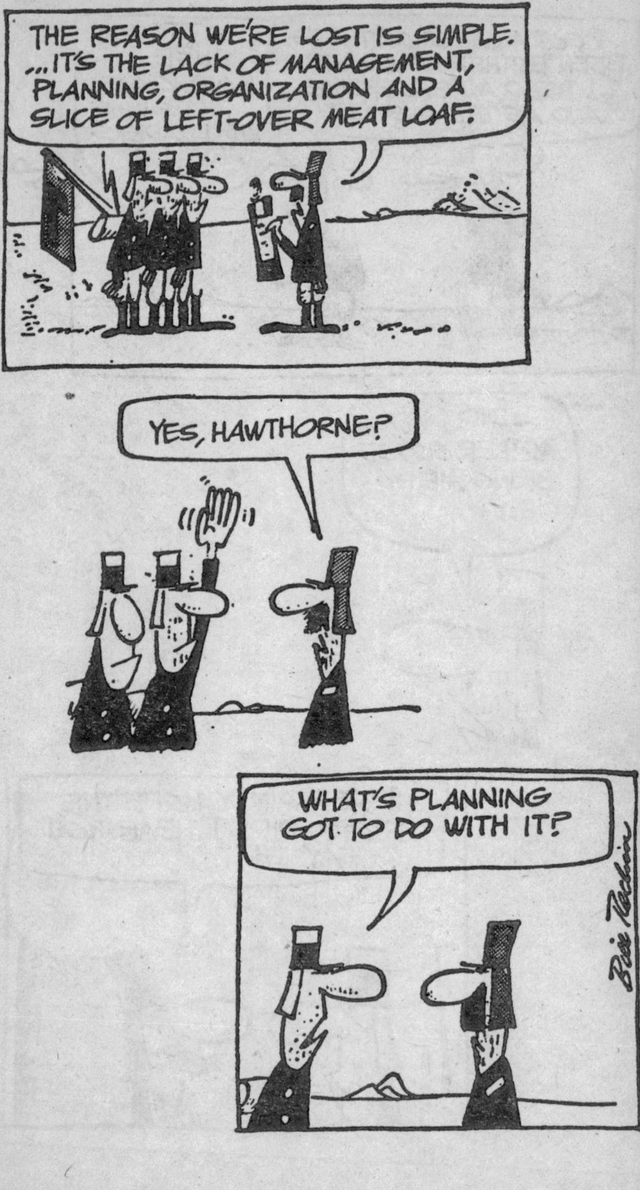
THE REASON WE'RE LOST IS SIMPLE. ...IT'S THE LACK OF MANAGEMENT, PLANNING, ORGANIZATION AND A SLICE OF LEFT-OVER MEAT LOAF.
YES, HAWTHORNE?
WHAT'S PLANNING GOT TO DO WITH IT?

monday

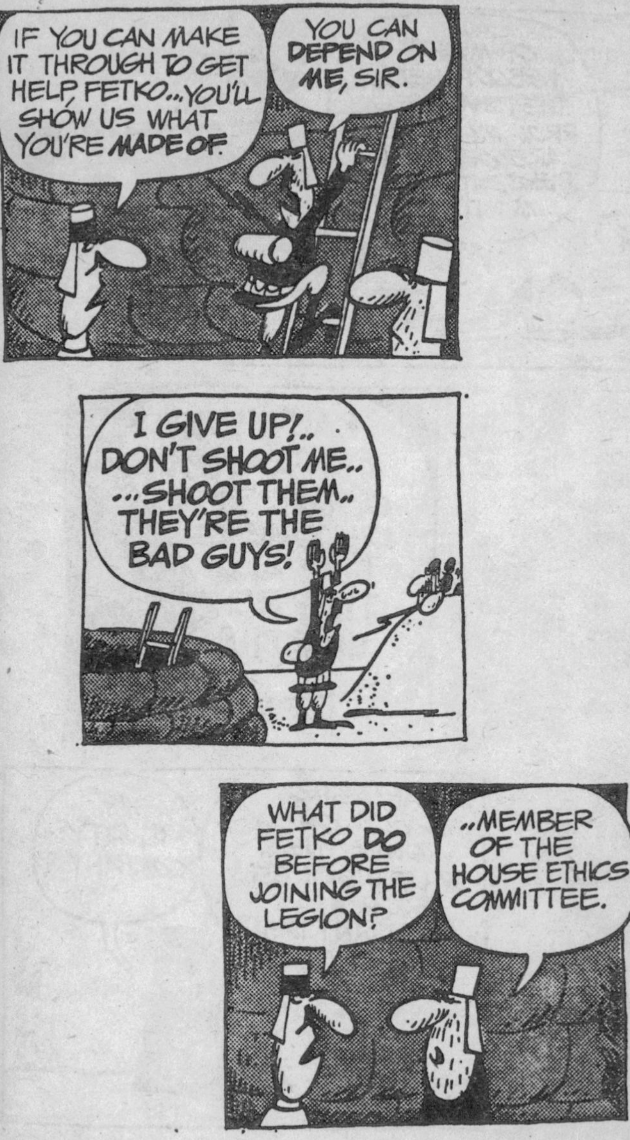
IF YOU CAN MAKE IT THROUGH TO GET HELP, FETKO...YOU'LL SHOW US WHAT YOU'RE MADE OF.
YOU CAN DEPEND ON ME, SIR.
I GIVE UP!.. DON'T SHOOT ME.. ...SHOOT THEM.. THEY'RE THE BAD GUYS!
WHAT DID FETKO DO BEFORE JOINING THE LEGION?
..MEMBER OF THE HOUSE ETHICS COMMITTEE.

tuesday

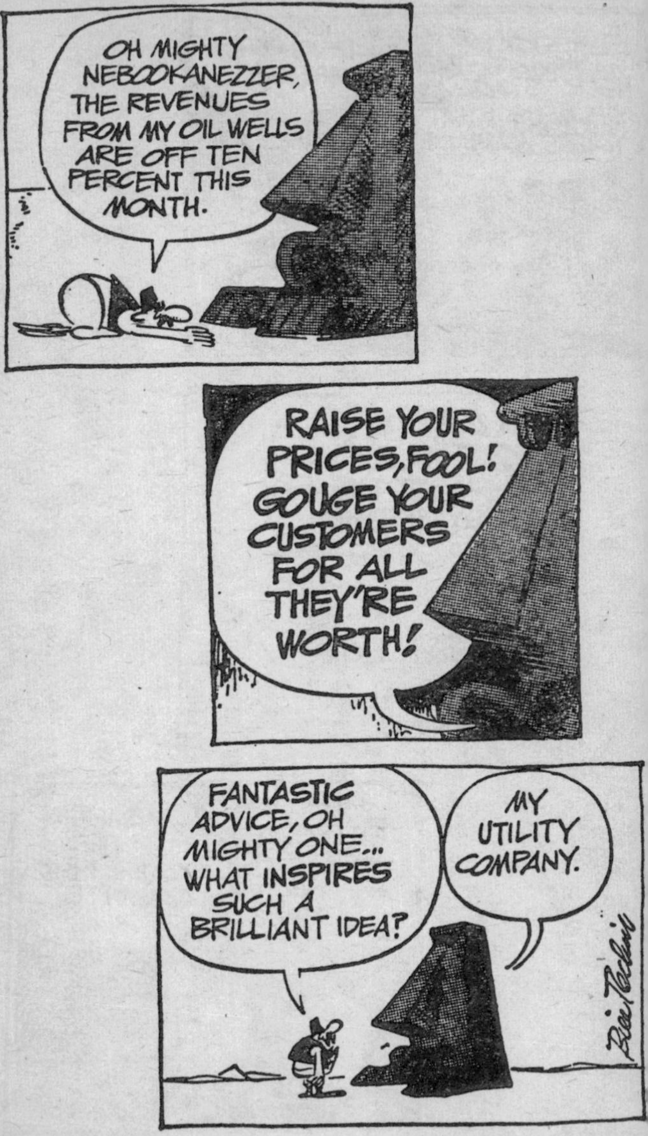
OH MIGHTY NEBOOKANEZZER, THE REVENUES FROM MY OIL WELLS ARE OFF TEN PERCENT THIS MONTH.
RAISE YOUR PRICES, FOOL! GOUGE YOUR CUSTOMERS FOR ALL THEY'RE WORTH!
FANTASTIC ADVICE, OH MIGHTY ONE... WHAT INSPIRES SUCH A BRILLIANT IDEA?
MY UTILITY COMPANY.

wednesday

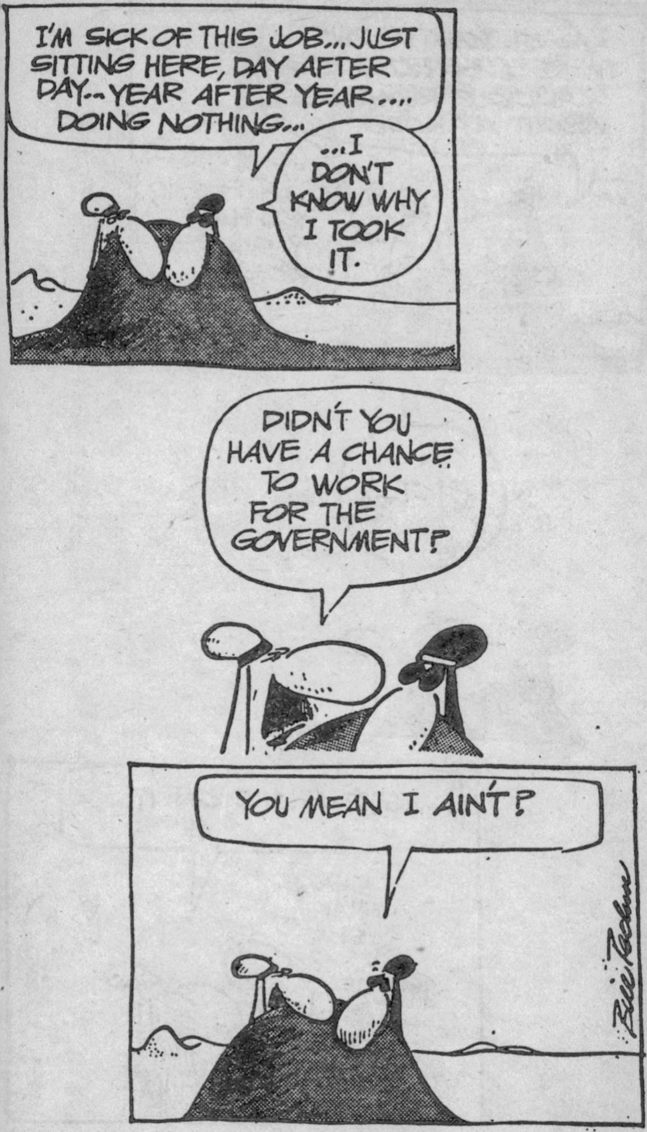

I'M SICK OF THIS JOB... JUST SITTING HERE, DAY AFTER DAY... YEAR AFTER YEAR.... DOING NOTHING...
...I DON'T KNOW WHY I TOOK IT.
DIDN'T YOU HAVE A CHANCE TO WORK FOR THE GOVERNMENT?
YOU MEAN I AIN'T?

thursday

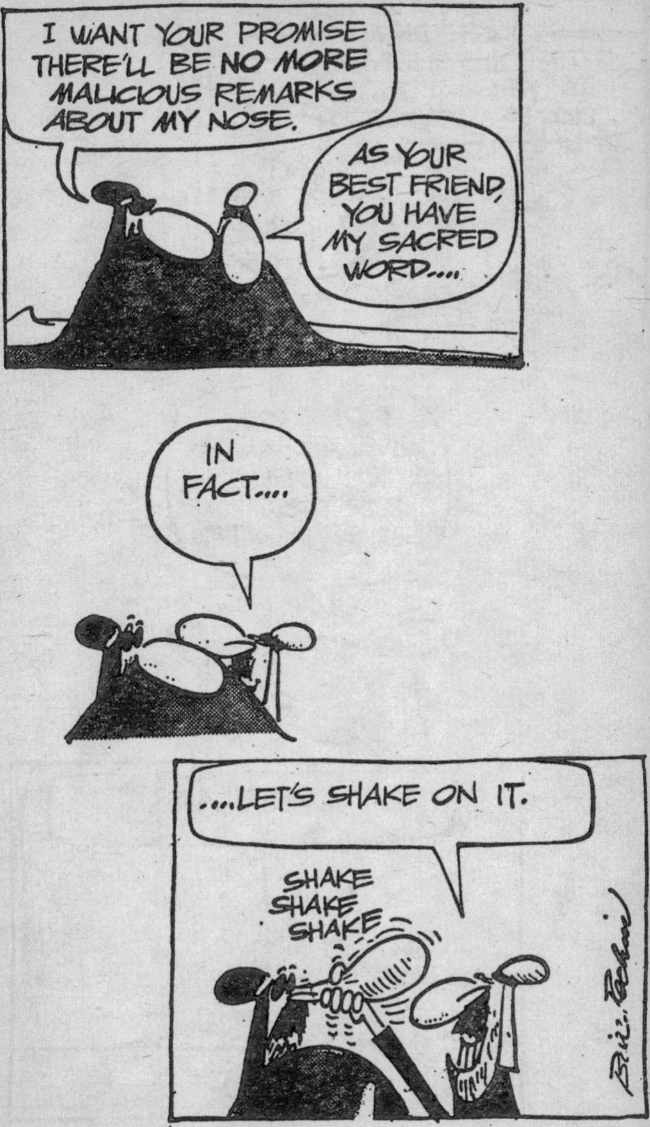
I WANT YOUR PROMISE THERE'LL BE NO MORE MALICIOUS REMARKS ABOUT MY NOSE.
AS YOUR BEST FRIEND, YOU HAVE MY SACRED WORD....
IN FACT....
....LET'S SHAKE ON IT.
SHAKE SHAKE SHAKE

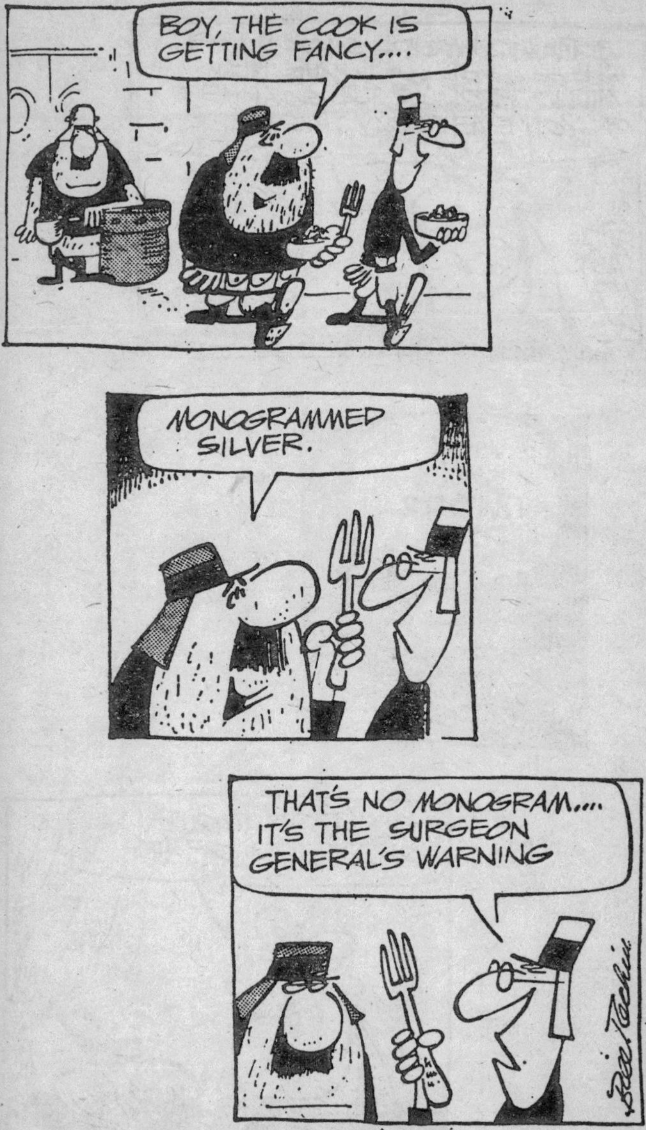
BOY, THE COOK IS GETTING FANCY....
MONOGRAMMED SILVER.
THAT'S NO MONOGRAM.... IT'S THE SURGEON GENERAL'S WARNING

saturday

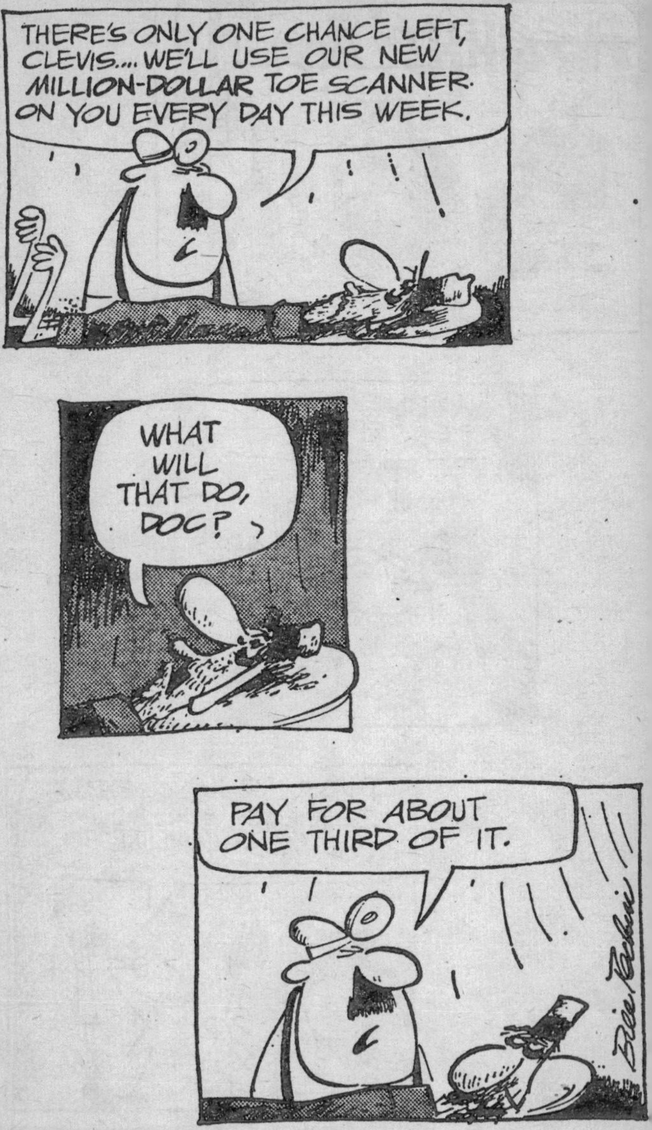
THERE'S ONLY ONE CHANCE LEFT, CLEVIS.... WE'LL USE OUR NEW MILLION-DOLLAR TOE SCANNER ON YOU EVERY DAY THIS WEEK.
WHAT WILL THAT DO, DOC?
PAY FOR ABOUT ONE THIRD OF IT.

monday

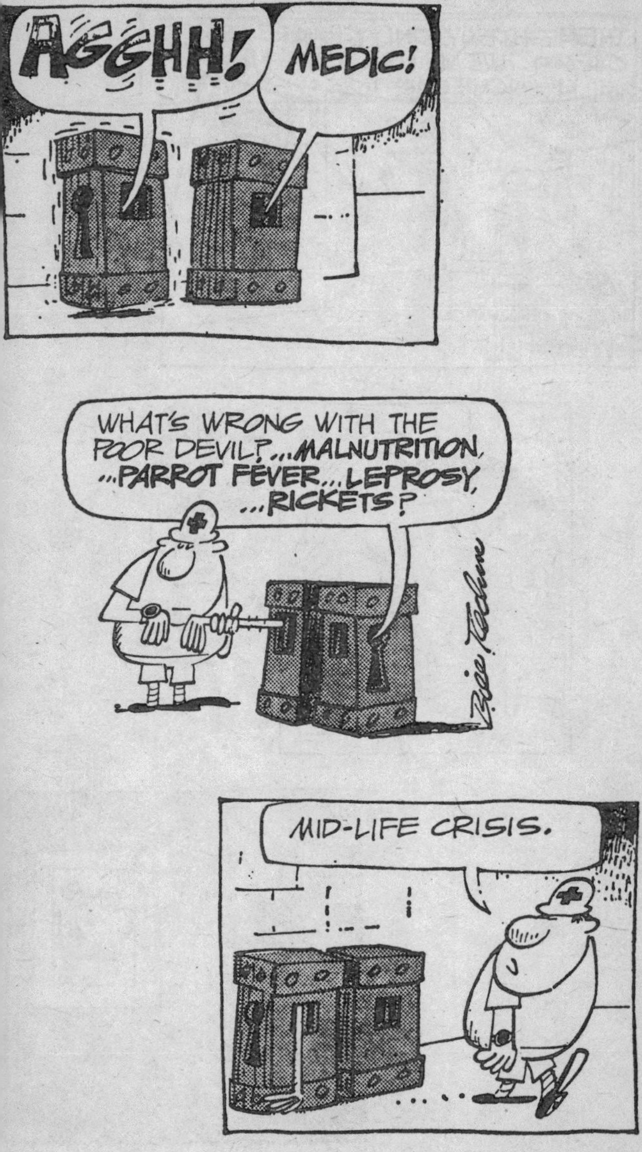
AGGHH!
MEDIC!
WHAT'S WRONG WITH THE POOR DEVIL?...MALNUTRITION, ...PARROT FEVER...LEPROSY, ...RICKETS?
MID-LIFE CRISIS.

tuesday

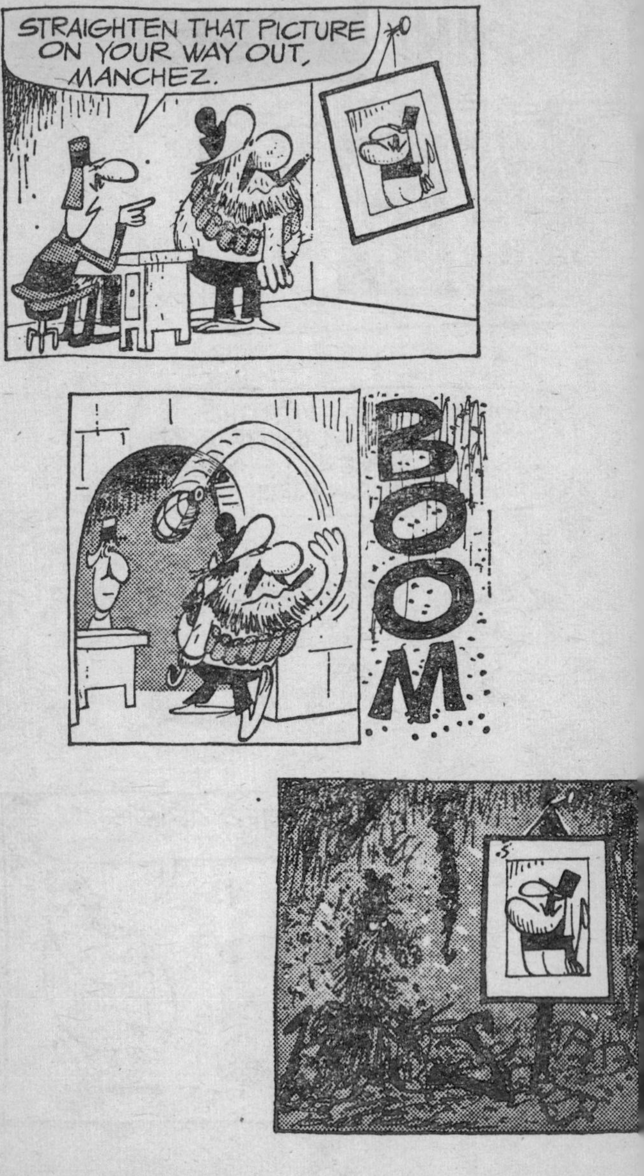
STRAIGHTEN THAT PICTURE ON YOUR WAY OUT, MANCHEZ.
BOOM

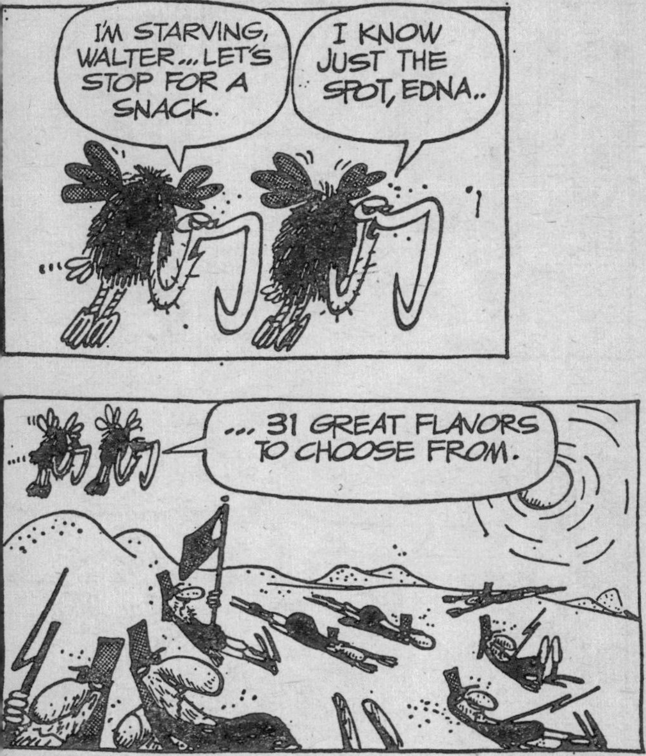
I'M STARVING, WALTER... LET'S STOP FOR A SNACK.
I KNOW JUST THE SPOT, EDNA..
... 31 GREAT FLAVORS TO CHOOSE FROM.

thursday

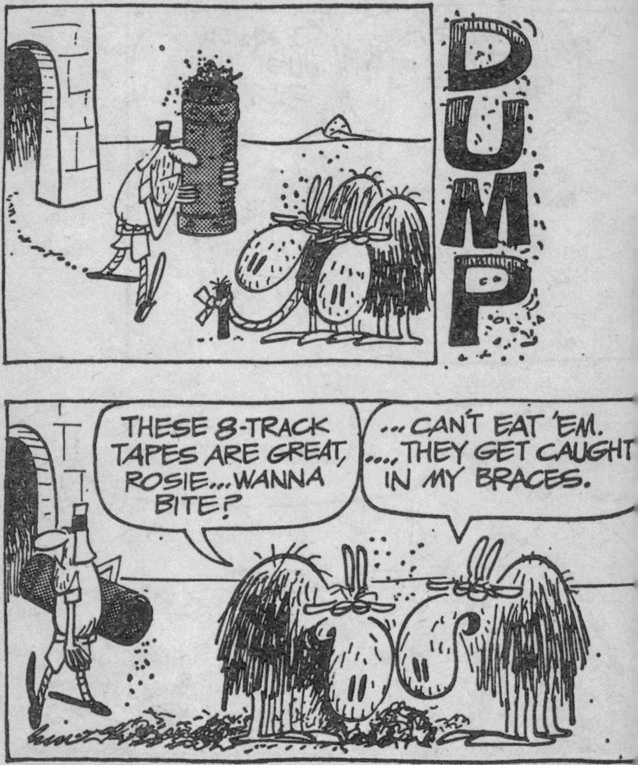
DUMP
THESE 8-TRACK TAPES ARE GREAT, ROSIE... WANNA BITE?
...CAN'T EAT 'EM. ..., THEY GET CAUGHT IN MY BRACES.

friday

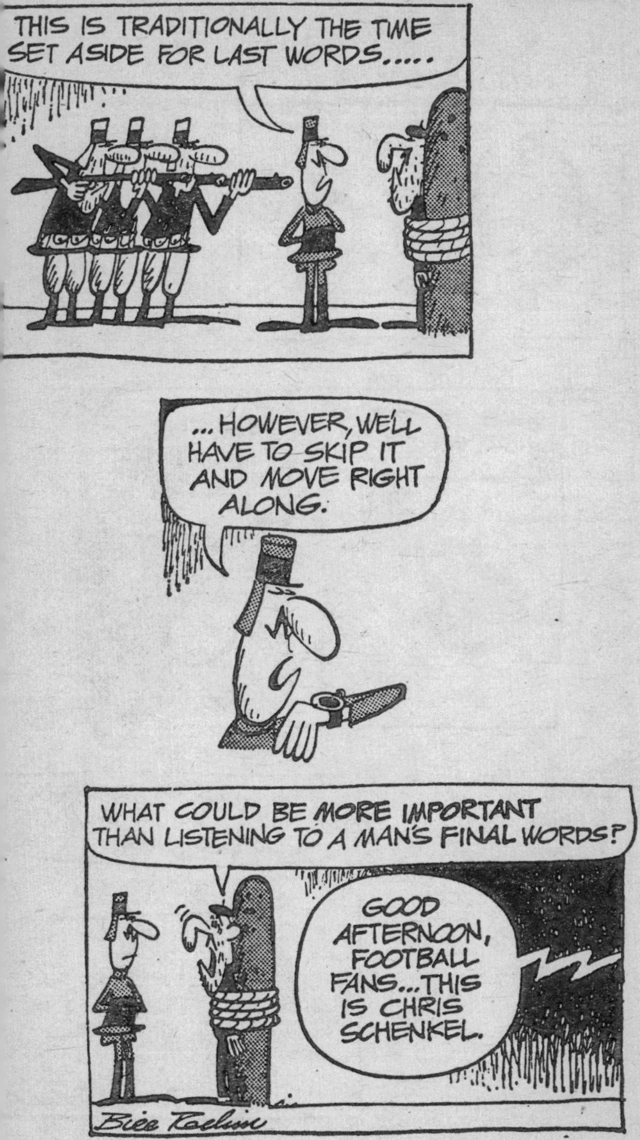
THIS IS TRADITIONALLY THE TIME SET ASIDE FOR LAST WORDS.....
...HOWEVER, WE'LL HAVE TO SKIP IT AND MOVE RIGHT ALONG.
WHAT COULD BE MORE IMPORTANT THAN LISTENING TO A MAN'S FINAL WORDS?
GOOD AFTERNOON, FOOTBALL FANS...THIS IS CHRIS SCHENKEL.

saturday

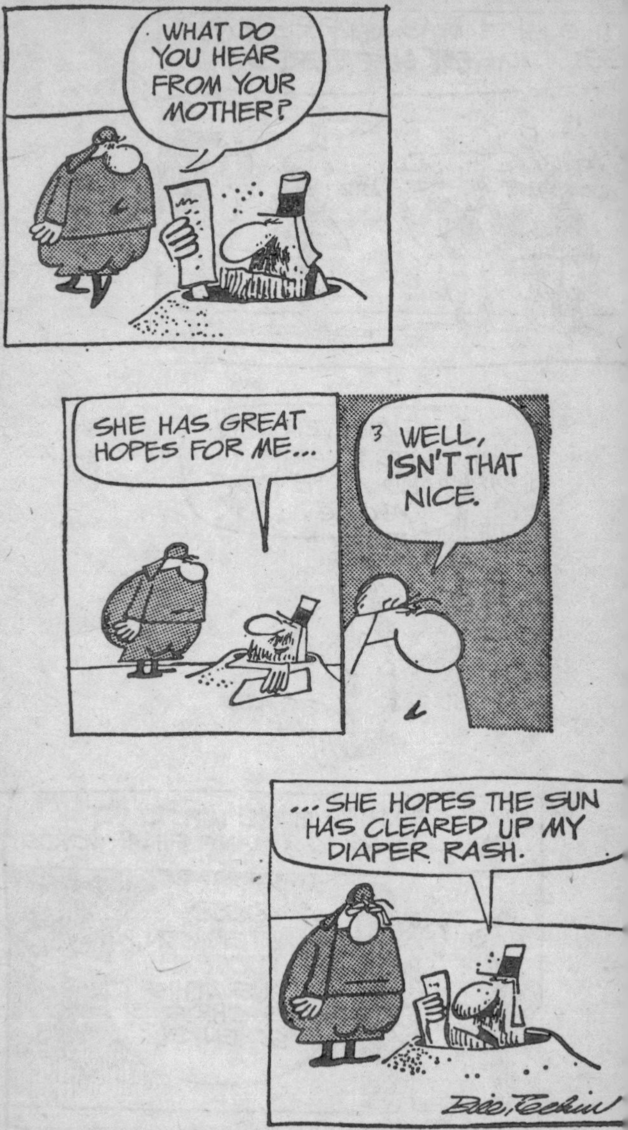
WHAT DO YOU HEAR FROM YOUR MOTHER?
SHE HAS GREAT HOPES FOR ME...
WELL, ISN'T THAT NICE.
...SHE HOPES THE SUN HAS CLEARED UP MY DIAPER RASH.

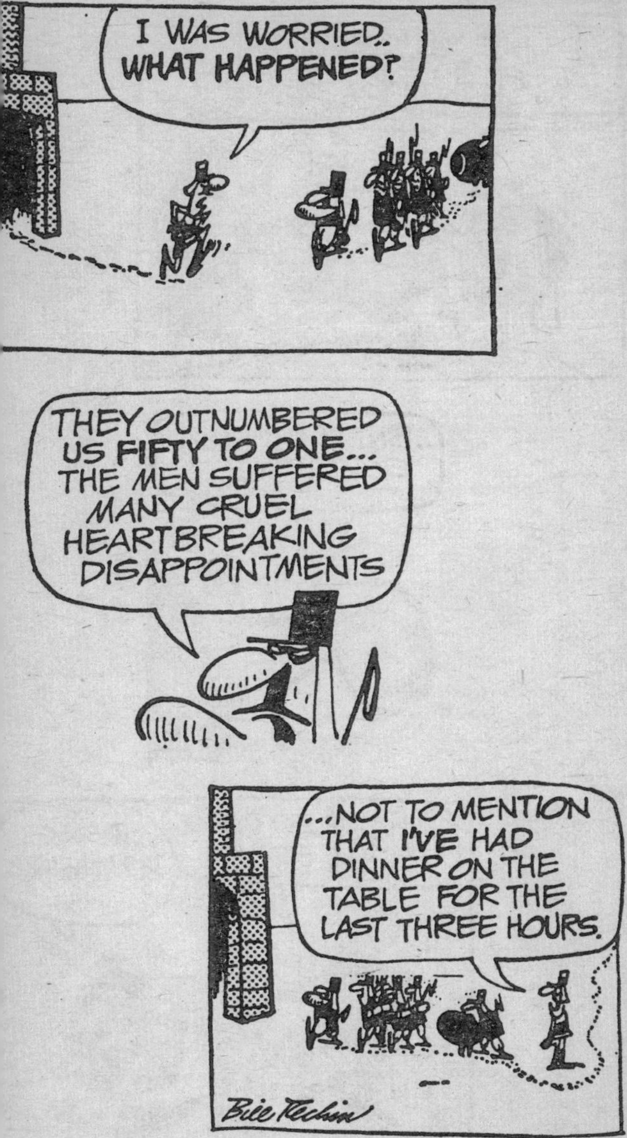
I WAS WORRIED.. WHAT HAPPENED?
THEY OUTNUMBERED US FIFTY TO ONE... THE MEN SUFFERED MANY CRUEL HEARTBREAKING DISAPPOINTMENTS
...NOT TO MENTION THAT I'VE HAD DINNER ON THE TABLE FOR THE LAST THREE HOURS.

tuesday

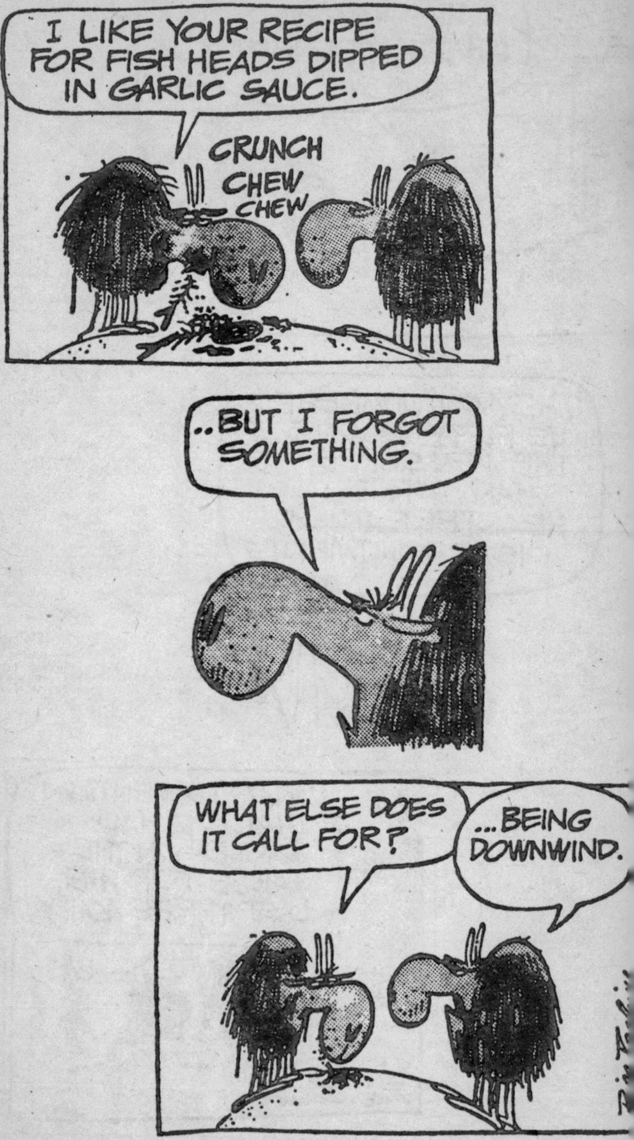
I LIKE YOUR RECIPE FOR FISH HEADS DIPPED IN GARLIC SAUCE.
CRUNCH
CHEW
CHEW
..BUT I FORGOT SOMETHING.
WHAT ELSE DOES IT CALL FOR?
...BEING DOWNWIND.

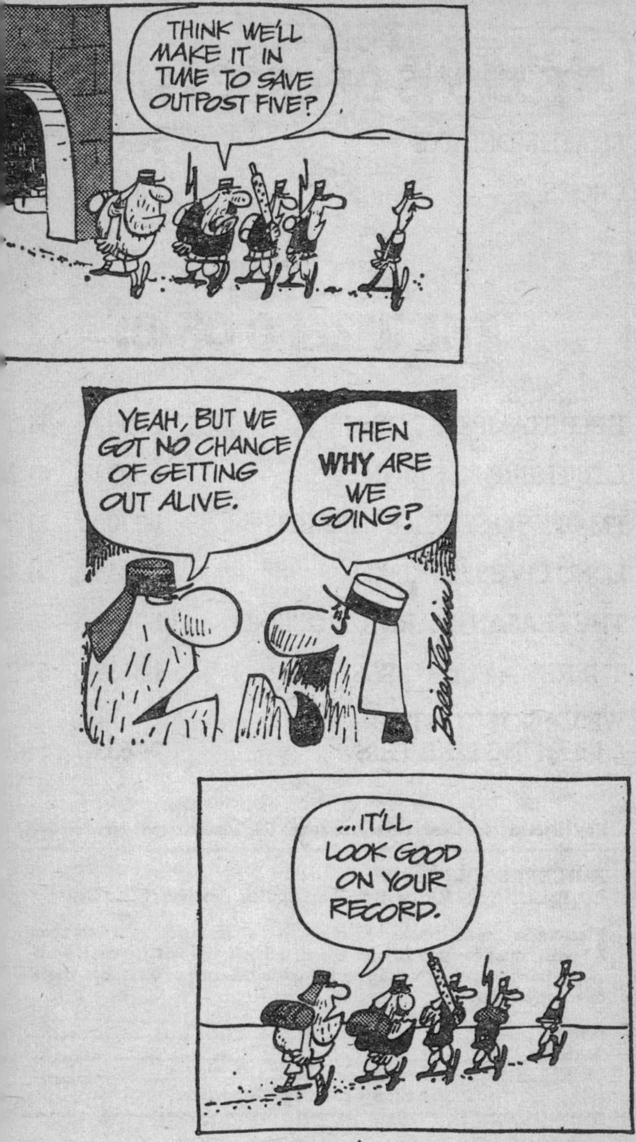
THINK WE'LL MAKE IT IN TIME TO SAVE OUTPOST FIVE?
YEAH, BUT WE GOT NO CHANCE OF GETTING OUT ALIVE.
THEN WHY ARE WE GOING?
Brian Tesla...
...IT'LL LOOK GOOD ON YOUR RECORD.

MORE FUN
FOR THE
LEGIONS OF CROCK FANS